Entering
the Diamond Way

TIBETAN BUDDHISM MEETS THE WEST

LAMA OLE NYDAHL

BLUE DOLPHIN

Dedicated to
the 17th Karmapa, THAYE DORJE,
my students and family

Original Title:
Die Buddhas vom Dach der Welt: Mein Weg zu den Lamas
Copyright © 1979 Eugen Diederichs Verlag, Köln
ISBN 3-424-00664

Når Jernfuglen Flyver
Copyright © 1983 Borgens Forlag
ISBN 87-418-5614-7

Copyright © 1985 Blue Dolphin Publishing Inc.
Entering the Diamond Way: My Path Among the Lamas

Copyright © 1999 Kamtsang Choling
Entering the Diamond Way: Tibetan Buddhism Meets the West
Blue Dolphin Publishing, Inc.
P.O. Box 8, Nevada City, CA 95959
Orders: 1-800-643-0765
Web site: http://www.bluedolphinpublishing.com

ISBN: 0-931892-03-1

LCCN: 85-73182

First printing, 1985
Revised edition, 1999

Index by Brackney Indexing Service
Cover photo: Michel van Dinteren / Amsterdam
Photo of Hannah & Ole Nydahl by Jason Langer / San Francisco

Printed in the United States of America by
Blue Dolphin Press, Grass Valley, California

5   4   3

Contents

D. C. CENTRE
RUMTEK, SIKKIM,
I N D I A .

H. H. SHAMARPA

11-8-1983

To Whom It May Concern.

This is to certify that Mr. Ole Nydahl, Denmark, is appoint-
ed Buddhist Master, and that he transmits the blessing and activity of the Karma Kagyud Lineage.

His qualifications are these: He has been a close, personal
disciple of H.H. the Gyalwa Karmapa since December 1969, when
he met Him at the Swayambhu Stupa in Nepal, and he has taken i-
nitiations and Mahamudra teachings from His Holiness and the
highest Kagyud Lamas which he has practiced accordingly.

For the last 10 years he has been starting centres, teaching
and protecting the practitioners all over the world on the request of His Holiness, and he is fully qualified in guiding meditations and leading people in the Dharma.

His wide-ranging activity has been of great benefit for countless students so far, and it is my request that Mr. Ole Nydahl
may be recognized in accordance with the above declaration and
receive all help in his important work.

His Holiness Shamarpa Rinpoche

Foreword

Dear Friends,

The 1999 edition of this book requires little introduction. Before it was to be translated into six East European languages as well as Dutch, I read it through for the first time since translating it in 1985. There is no doubt that my English has improved since then and that is what you benefit from here. In addition I clarified some fuzzy meanings and added a few updates to avoid loose ends. There also now exists the sequel, *Riding the Tiger*, about the first twenty years of starting the Diamond Way around the world and Tomek Lehnert's *Rogues in Robes* about recent Chinese influences on Tibetan Buddhism, both published by Blue Dolphin Publishing.

My thanks to Carol Aronoff for the first edition and to Sarah Kalff and Charlotte Weber, Stewart Jarvis and Hannah for helping this time,

Yours
TCH and Lama Ole
Perth, Western Australia.
Dakini Day in Protector month, February 1999

CHAPTER ONE

Our Honeymoon Journey

CHOOSING NEPAL FOR OUR HONEYMOON in the summer of 1968 was no bad idea. It was the very time in history when the early and still idealistic Hippie scene of Europe and the old schools of Tibetan Buddhism could meet, giving direction to the former and a chance for the latter not to end up in museums but survive as a living practice. Years of traveling the worn paths between the green lowlands of Northern Europe and the icy peaks of the Himalayas would follow, bringing forth lay and yogic Diamond Way Buddhism as it thrives today. For the first time in history, the meeting of Western idealism and intelligent Asian materialism now combine vast and formerly untried aspects of mind's potential.

As my lovely wife Hannah, myself, and later so many fine friends discovered, what appeared was a tool to master life. The Diamond Way expertly transforms disturbed states of consciousness into most enjoyable clarity and bliss. In a completely practical way, it makes every aspect of life useful towards liberation and enlightenment.

In the exciting company of co-smugglers and other adventurous friends during those years, it was possible to spend real time with the highest Tibetan and Bhutanese lamas. Their examples and exceedingly skillful teachings inspired us, and after a careful examination they chose us as partners in bringing their powerful transmissions and meditations into the West.

The main aim of this book is to recount what happened when the best of two so different but valuable cultures met. Its continuation,

Riding the Tiger, will describe the following maturation of the work. It may have been the only case in history when experienced people from two advanced civilizations so consciously tried to learn the best from each other. With the tragic losses of the last years, during which several of the old lamas holding a full inner and secret transmission have died, it feels good to reprint a book that shares the atmosphere of that first encounter.

Hannah was twenty-two and I twenty-seven when we first met living Diamond Way Buddhism. Our parents were teachers at colleges in the residential areas north of Copenhagen. They were precious people, and we grew up in a world full of confidence in the fundamental goodness of man. Though we were raised in a completely humanistic setting from earliest childhood, I had recurrent, exciting dreams of war in mountain areas which I had never seen. In them, I beat back round-faced soldiers and protected what I could then only understand as men in red, ladies' clothes. Not until 25 years later, when I saw the first Tibetan monks in Nepal, did I understand what they were, and only 45 years later, on a secret tour through Chinese-occupied eastern Tibet, did I see the mountains and villages which I had fought to protect.

Also in this life, I automatically fought anything bigger—be it people or systems—that would limit my freedom. Hannah was just as independent but worked with things inwardly instead of bashing the outer world.

In the autumn of 1961, when I was discharged from compulsory military service (the army would have loved to get rid of me sooner), I was one of the first Danes to smoke "pot," as we called it then, the plant product which has since been called everything from grass to laughing-weed. At the time, I had just passed philosophy with the best marks, and anything having to do with mind always aroused a burning interest in me. I expected countless new insights from this, and later mind altering drugs, and allowed them to give direction to the next years of my life. As I thought they markedly benefited sentient beings, I decided to write my doctorate on Aldous Huxley and his *Doors of Perception.*

While I spent the next few years studying in Denmark and Germany, adding boxing and motorcycle accidents to the chemical attacks on my brain, Hannah worked her way through the last years of high school.

We met again at that place of so many encounters, the eatery at the university of Copenhagen called "The Cannibal." When I was ten and Hannah was five, I had shown her how to build huts from branches in the woods in the northern suburbs. Although girls don't climb trees well and for that reason rated low on my scale, still I walked her home. For the first time in this life, I had apparently fallen in love. Shortly after, however, her parents moved further north, and we lost contact. Now, nearly fifteen years later, she stood in front of me again, unbelievably beautiful and even making me forget the exciting, red-haired lady at my side. Although she had then been engaged for four years, soon we were living together.

On my twenty-fifth birthday, in March of 1966, I had my first experience with LSD. Returning to our party by the now very changed streets of medieval Copenhagen, I felt drawn through a narrow gate and into a courtyard lit by a single lantern. I knew some very special experience was waiting there. Stopping before a house with deep, empty windows, I heard myself saying to it, "Now, show me everything." The moving, breathing quality of my surroundings increased, and whirls of luminous white light closed in. It felt as if the energies of a whole universe were flooding into me and exploding into space. A timeless, radiant intensity pervaded everywhere. Coming back to the party, I could only say, "I'm not sure what it was, but everything is all right."

Shortly after, Hannah joined me in mapping these other levels of consciousness. Here again, her experiences were always deep and warm. Beginning with twenty to thirty friends—the first cohesive group in northern Europe—we tried all the mind-changing drugs coming out during those years but apparently without learning much: We could still believe in their ability to illuminate and benefit, while the bodies and minds of our best friends were breaking down from their use. I would give anything to have them all back with us today, but most have already died—usually in really unpleasant ways—while a few are so lost in their private universes that there is no place left to contact them in this life. Today we have only one piece of advice about drugs: stay away from them. Drugs rob our subconscious, leaving people empty. The damage, which does not appear at once, will come later and is difficult to repair. To reach enlightenment, only one's natural mind is needed as it is here and now, together with the right methods.

At that time I was teaching English at an evening college. During the frequent holidays, we made short trips to North Africa, Lebanon, and Afghanistan to bring back hash for our friends. While north of Bombay on a flight to Indonesia in 1967 (still nauseated from a recent bout of hepatitis and carrying thirty-four kilos of gold in a waistcoat which was much too tight), I saw luminous cloud formations coming down from the Himalayas. They were of such beauty and made such a deep impression on me that I suddenly knew we had to go to where these clouds were coming from. Something was waiting for us there, something important.

In May 1968, Hannah and I married, the wisest thing we had done so far. She was twenty-two and I was twenty-seven as we went on our honeymoon trip to Nepal. I had been on my way there overland in 1966, but a war between India and Pakistan had stopped everybody in Afghanistan for three weeks, long enough to pick up the most evil dysentery in Asia. Fifty-five pounds lighter, hitchhiking and walking, with no money and selling my blood at hospitals along the way back to Europe, was an interesting experience.

This time we did not want any stops on the way. The day my students passed their exam, we got into an old Volkswagen bus and a used VW beetle waiting in Hamburg and just drove south. Claes and Christian, who had provided my first pot, and his wife also came along. Christian was now in a wheelchair. He had jumped out of a window on a "trip" and had broken his back, which left only Hannah, Claes, and myself to drive the cars. Claes, however, soon had enough of the 55-degree centigrade temperatures through Iran, the dust everywhere, and the unpaved washboard, which then served as the road through the desert. However, we would give anything to reach Nepal as quickly as possible. After a record six days and nights, we crossed into Afghanistan. Christian and his wife wanted to stay with the knockout hash in Kabul, so we dropped them off and quickly sold our bus at a price that financed our whole tour. Hardly was this done when Hannah repeated my experience of two years earlier. She came down with an evil diarrhea, luckily in a hotel with a toilet. The next

Trading in Kabul, 1968

day, filled with antibiotics, I carried her on a bus going further east. It would take us down the Khyber Pass onto the northern plains of Pakistan and India.

While in Kabul, we had met some Danes restoring the largest Buddha in the world. Fifty-three meters tall, it stands a day's bus ride north of Kabul at Bamian. It is one of the cultural treasures which in 1996 the Muslim Taleban vowed to destroy for not being Islamic. It may still happen if they conquer the northern part of Afghanistan. These Danes were experts on what was left of the formerly rich Buddhist culture of the area. Although much had been damaged already a thousand years ago when Moslems knocked the noses off the statues to take away their power, during the late sixties there was still a lot to see. After the time of Alexander the Great, 300 BC, the Gandhara culture blossomed here. Its art is easily recognizable by the Buddhas with mustaches, showing a mixture of Greek and Indian elements, which followed his conquest of the area. The Peshawar museum in Pakistan contains an impressive collection, and it was odd to see recently captured Indian guns displayed proudly in the middle of this otherwise well-researched collection from the time of the English.

It was good to get to India. Already at the border we felt the difference. Leaving behind the tense, sexually frustrated atmosphere of the Moslem countries, where I had to push people away from

Hannah regularly, was a true relief. Ferozepur was the next town with a train-connection to New Delhi. At that time, one had to get visas for Nepal there, while now they give one-week permits at the border. New Delhi is a town where people go for their papers, but no tourist stays longer than necessary. Only nearby Old Delhi has that picturesque Indian Ocean of sense impressions—mainly noise these days—which some Westerners enjoy, at least as long as they have enough money and thus the liberty to move on. Whoever cannot leave these masses of staring people must develop great patience.

In Delhi we had our first experience with Hindu gurus, a meeting that made us want our school money back but never touched our depths. We never felt a bond with them nor did we want one; they were much too personal and sweet. Nevertheless we had an impressive demonstration of some powers which their methods produce. It happened in Connaught Circus, the administrative center which the English left the Indians as a parting gift; it is said to confuse them ever more.

From this central point, with restaurants and tourist shops, streets radiate out to embassies and villas. Whatever then happened in New Delhi, happened here. While walking under the arcades, an old Indian with a turban stepped in front of us. He mumbled something about "lucky forehead" and put three pieces of rolled up paper in my hand. Gesturing in front of my face, he drew my attention to his hands. At the same time he looked straight into my eyes and asked me

India seen from the train

to give the name of a fruit. I was thinking of a whole row of fruits, some of which he had probably never heard of, but while I was still wondering if I could play a joke on an old man like him, I had already said "apple." He looked very happy, took one of the pieces of paper from my hand, opened it, and that was what it said. "Now, name a flower," he pressed, and again more or less the same thing happened. While still thinking of hibiscus and other exotic plants, in that half trance-like, half-conscious state of hypnotic influence, the idea and the picture of a rose appeared, and in order not to disturb the interesting course of events, I said, "rose."

Of course it said "rose" on the second piece of paper, which made him jump around even more. For the third test, however, where I was to mention a number between one and ten, my pride only allowed me to think of the number "one," and I just held onto that, blocking all outer influences. His luck held, however. The "seven" which he had tried to suggest into my mind and which was on the remaining slip looked so much like a one that he was able to save the situation, and we could continue with the game. We followed him around a corner to where no policemen could see him, and opening the book, which many soothsayers carry around with them, he said, "Put money in it, and I will tell you the future."

As northern Europeans, where churches are supported by taxation, we didn't like money and spirituality so openly together. Since the Nepalese embassy was closing, however, and also out of compassion for this old man who was working so hard, we put the equivalent of two dollars in his book as a gift. Hannah kept saying we must leave, and as his power over the situation weakened and he felt he could not hold us anymore, he showed us as a parting gift that he could do more than suggest ideas into people's minds. He told us that a girl named Jensen had talked about us to the police at home. At that time it meant nothing to us, as we knew the last names of only few friends, but later we heard that a woman of that same name had grassed about us to the police. So apparently the old man really had some clarity of vision. In parting he told me, as wise people frequently do, that I should stay with Hannah.

From the time we left Copenhagen, a green book with an athletic-looking Buddha on the cover had been our steady companion. We dug into it every free minute we had. Its name was *Tibetan Yoga and*

*Entering Nepal
the first time,
typical houses*

*Terraced rice-fields
on way to
Kathmandu Valley*

Secret Doctrines, and it was translated by the Lama Kazi Dawa Samdup and edited by the English scholar Evans-Wentz. It contains very intense and effective practices of the Kagyu School of Tibetan Buddhism, which the Buddha had told only to his closest students. Whenever we opened the book, the reading produced strong experiences in us, states we had hardly known before. We felt a special warmth, a happiness, and deep longing. While the sensation of a half pleasant but also overwhelming and painful tingling energy moved upwards in the center of my body, an inner voice repeated ever more intensely, "We are coming; we are really coming now." All the way from Hamburg this voice had been in my mind, and now so close to our goal, we nearly exploded with impatience. Hardly were the visas in our pockets than we boarded the train to Nepal.

The ride from Delhi to Raxaul, a town from where one crosses over into Birgunj in Nepal and catches a bus to Kathmandu, was our first experience of northeastern Indian trains. Whoever has not tried this cannot imagine what it is like. Hundreds of yelling, white-clad fellow humans force their way into the wagons at every station until people nearly fall out of the windows, and even the roofs of the carriages fill to capacity. It is really amazing that physical violence is so rare in the intense heat and constant jostling. At first everyone screams and yells; that is a part of the ritual, but once the train is rolling again, there are no hard feelings till the next stop when the wave of humanity starts pushing its way in once more.

Of all the states of India, Bihar is the one hardest hit by all sorts of natural catastrophes. Year after year, either floods or droughts destroy the crops, and also the mental climate is very rough. Local people think that even the spirits of their dead mothers are liable to turn against them and have special protectors made against them.

The transition into the beautiful foothills of Nepal is thus a change on many levels. One here crosses over into the "other" world where the mountain-people live. Already in Patna, while on the boat on the Ganges River, we had seen the first small and muscular Nepalese, often Gurkha soldiers on their way home. They were islands of peace in an ocean of noise and disturbance. In them, we felt a very attractive wholeness. As the lowlands of India and its confused multitudes disappeared behind us and the green hills were everywhere, this feeling of peace grew until it enveloped us. We felt at ease among these people where a woman can move alone freely and naturally without being in danger. Here the women looked into one's face and laughed and joked. After the scarves, veiled faces, and walking tents of the Moslem countries and the Indian women who are expert at avoiding any contact, they provided a much-missed feeling of openness. Although many had told us that we would be cheated in whatever dealings we had with them, we did not even notice it at first. After all, it was only a question of a few pennies. Anyway, in the beginning nobody can decipher the value of the small brass and aluminum coins. They are covered on both sides with good-luck symbols but carry no numbers. One's discovery, however, that even matchboxes are officially sealed to keep the contents from disappearing on their way to the buyer, helped us to adjust to their ways. As our business transactions became more insisting, we achieved a much closer contact with the people. Now for the first time they took us seriously.

The monsoon rains had started as we entered India, and the road which leads from Birgunj over the foothills to Kathmandu had already been washed away in several places. In the Himalayas, the yearly repair of these roads is the only certain source of work for the locals, and this is one convincing reason for not doing the mending too well. For double insurance, they leave huge rocks at strategic points on the mountainsides. With a gentle prodding at the right time they can be made to slide down, thus insuring more income. Earning at best about half a dollar a day, they are not very open to the idea of luxuriously long holidays.

In an age-old, noisy, and shaking bus, totally overloaded like all means of transportation in this part of the world, we slowly rattled up into the mountains, taking in all we could. One thing we liked, and got used to quickly, was that in every dangerous situation—and there are many on that road—both the driver and the passengers spontaneously laughed or smiled. We understood it as a timeless method for not losing face while preventing impressions of fear from solidifying in their minds and were impressed by the practical wisdom of it. While dusk made things seem even more otherworldly, this country blessed by so many Buddhas now received us.

It was still the good old days in Kathmandu. The country had just been opened to foreigners a few years earlier, and there were hardly any tourists. Even the streams of hippies had not yet arrived. Whoever ran down a cow in a Hindu area easily risked his neck. If he could not prove (often by donations in the right places) that the animal, a god to the Hindus, had decided to commit suicide in front of his car, he was in big trouble. Two or three sturdy old taxis, among them an ancient Volvo which never had to be repaired, were the forerunners of the countless dented Datsuns and Toyotas today.

Constantly in too high a gear to save gas, and always hooting, they wind their way through the narrow passages of Kathmandu and really show the difference between cultures: the local coolies, pushcarts, bicyclists, and pedestrians make room with angel-like patience while all tourists are outraged by the noise. Then as now, one could drink

*Nepalese procession,
Kathmandu*

only boiled liquids and eat only self-pealed fruit if one wanted to avoid hosting countless exotic microbes. On most evenings people from the culture-bearing Newari tribe would meet in the countless temples to chant ancient Buddhist meditation texts. They accompanied them by the drawn-out tones of their hand organs and sharp sounding drums, a music that went straight inside and made a powerful impact. Walking the historical streets, people's minds found peace and things happened soon after one thought of them. When, for example, we started out to visit friends, we usually met them on the way, saying, "Hello, I was just coming to see you." Often we held the desired object in our hands before having had the time to even formulate a clear wish, and it never ceased to bring a feeling of amazed joy. The many Buddhist temples, hundreds of years old, and the unbroken lineages of Buddhist yogis are the cause. They have created a field of power over the Kathmandu Valley that makes one's habitual separation between mind and matter much less binding. Also the chemistry was not lacking. At that time hash, the strongest and clearest acting in the world, could be bought legally from the state merchants. One leisurely tested the quality upstairs while the merchant's daughter brought tea, chatting about expectations for the next harvest. Today, the stuff is frequently low-grade and mixed with other substances, and due to the moralistic Americans paying off the Nepalese government, it is prohibited—at least officially.

The late sixties were also the time of colorful originals, such as "Eight Finger Eddie," an Armenian who made magical signs at a tea place called The Cabin. He had a strong influence on many of the long-haired hopefuls in Kathmandu, and soon his own school of freaks had sprung up, easily recognizable by their mustaches and sign language. There was also "Uncle," a blown-away Indian who gave away hash cakes improved with Morning Glory extract. After enjoying one, many a sweet tooth did not find his body again for several days. And then, of course, the good doctor around the corner who was always happy to help with a quick fix. While finding a still functioning vein, he praised the absolute sterility of his instruments and suggested that after this Chinese heroin, next time one should try his Burmese cocaine. It was of very special quality. He never gave anybody more than one shot a day and claimed to keep people below the level of addiction. When, however, we met his customers on their early morning walk to him, they seemed to be in quite a hurry. When we tried to engage them in a short chat, they shifted from one foot to the other, trying to get away as soon as they could. There was no mistaking the heavy, bad feeling of junkies. Maybe the good doctor thought he was just giving them a small daily pleasure, like a trip to the cinema, but actually they were getting hooked. Either he was not alone in the market, or people were weaker than he thought.

In those days, Peter Seller's films were prohibited because he looked too much like the King. Religious feasts and processions of one kind or another ran constantly. Once the whole town went on strike, shocked by the murder of a taxi-driver. Everyone was used to the daily cheating and even a few political murders were nothing new, but armed robbery (killing people outright for money!) was previously unknown. Most days brought new reasons for celebrating, and somewhere in the streets one always found people wearing garlands, playing music, and walking in processions past other groups carrying dead bodies on stretchers to the burning place by the river. It lies next to the slaughter place, where mainly Moslems work. They do the butchering in so much of Asia because, according to their religion, killing animals is not wrong.

Houses are small in Kathmandu, and average-sized northern Europeans like Hannah and I are giants there. In the old town, we could not stand in most rooms, and often we could not stretch out either. The windows are without glass but decorated with beautiful wood carvings, and the walls and ceilings are usually blackened with soot from the open fireplaces. Only the clay floors are always fresh and new. As soon as they become dirty or broken, they smear a thin new layer on top.

Everywhere in the old part of Kathmandu, as well as in the neighboring towns of Patan and Bhatgaon, we were surrounded by so much beauty and history that it felt like living in an impressive art exhibit. Especially outstanding were the omnipresent stupas. These are Buddhist relic shrines of special proportions, and like the images in the temples, they are constructed to activate one's inborn Buddha-essence by their mere presence. If one is not frightened away by the smells, the beggars, and sick people in the streets, their imprint on the mind will bring future states of insight and joy.

Many Danes had established themselves in colorful Kathmandu, and the amusing and "human" events of those years are just being discovered as material for several doctor's theses today. Here, I will relate only one incident to give the general feeling. It is about Niels, a skillful dealer who had adopted the religion and full garb of a Hindu saddhu, appearing in light-brown robes and sporting an iron trident which reached above his head. One day in Pashupathinath, the holiest Hindu place in Nepal, his colleagues suddenly discovered this Danish

Example of Buddhist art, Kathmandu

Bodhnath Stupa　　　　*Joy state Buddha at Swayambhu*

import. They yelled "American!", beat him up, and threw him out. The next day in Kathmandu market, one could pick up a Saddhu outfit, complete with trident and bowl, at a bargain price. Meanwhile, Niels was seen in sneakers and jeans on his way into a new trip.

After reading the book, *Tibetan Yoga and Secret Doctrines*, we were, of course, very eager to meet a Lama. The first "Lama" we met in Kathmandu, however, amazed us quite a bit. His name was Chinni Lama ("Chinni" means "Chinese" in the local language), and he lived in the pink house with the terrace across from the main entrance to the Bodhnath Stupa. His rate for dollars was twice that of the bank, and some friends had told us to change with him. We noticed a few fine Mercedes cars in the front of his house but didn't pay much attention at the time. Not till later were we told that his "Lama" title had been inherited and that his function was really one of caretaker of the Bodhnath Stupa—a job he seemed to manage well and certainly at no personal loss.

The Chinni Lama was a small and elderly, heavy-set man. He was bald and had very Chinese features. As we entered his room, he appeared to be just awakening. As he sat up slowly, with wonder we noticed at least five watches on each of his arms, from the wrist to above the elbows. It looked funny, but due to his title we told each other that he probably used them for very complicated breathing exercises. He at once asked us if we had any guns to sell, and we were touched that this compassionate man must be helping the Tibetan resistance fighters, the Khampas, whose righteous cause we supported. With regret we told him that we had no weapons, only the knives that we always carried. Then he wanted to know if we had any tape recorders. We did have the first Phillips model. Cassette recorders had just arrived on the market at that time, but having managed to bring one all the way East still in working order, we told him that we wanted to record some Tibetan temple music with it first. We were sure that this interest in Buddhism would delight him, but if it did, he hid it well.

Finding nothing to buy, he wanted to sell us some opium. We were highly amazed at this "holy" man's innocence. We insistently explained to him that opium is addictive, that it's unhealthy, that he should not sell it to people, and that it was slowly killing lots of our friends. At the same time, however, his words strengthened an illusion which we were not to give up until several years later, namely that all "holy" people in the East were taking some kind of drugs. Finally, the Chinni Lama sold us some overpriced hash but changed our dollars at a fantastic rate.

Later that evening, when testing the stuff with friends in a tearoom in town, we soon rolled on our backs with laughter. The expensive, three-dollar, first-sized piece of hash proved to be charcoal covered with black shoe polish—a lesson that one should check the merchandise even in the best of company.

There was much to do in Kathmandu, lots to see and experience. What especially attracted us, however, was the hill with the Swayambhu temple on top, somewhat outside town. The shortest way there takes one past the heaped-up skulls of newly butchered animals and the most well nourished but rabid gangs of dogs in the valley. The area one passes through feels dirty, and one did not stop at the teahouses, which probably get their water from the nearby river. Neither these unpleasant factors nor the transcendental charms of town were important. Day after day we traversed the area, drawn by the magic hill.

From Kathmandu, the Swayambhu Temple is visible on top of a pyramid-like hill. Steep steps lead there from three directions, weaving among large Buddha-statues and countless stupas. The symbolic form of stupas represent the five wisdoms realized at Buddhahood and thus inherent in all sentient beings. The hill's top is a central dome from the time of the third Buddha Oesung (Sanskrit: *Mahakasha*). He was active in our world before the historical Buddha Sakyamuni, whose teachings are with us now. This impressive building is the main seat in Nepal of the great Tibetan yogi Gyalwa Karmapa and his main lineage-holder, Kunzig Shamarpa, who were later to become so important to us.

Around the dome is a ring-like yard. Visitors walk it clockwise, saying mantras, and those who don't find the prayer wheels too greasy, set them in motion with their hands. After several brick buildings follows the gray-white Tibetan monastery with a majestic central entrance to the altar.

The Nepali word *Swayambhu* means the "self-originated" place. For the Buddhists of this region it is as holy as Bodh Gaya in India, where Buddha Sakyamuni manifested Full Enlightenment. As the Indians frequently pester visitors, many can more easily open up in Nepal. In addition, the area had a very perceptible power field. It enhances meditation and brings all wishes to quick maturation.

Our first impression, however, was decidedly poor. We neither liked the dirt, which, like most places in Nepal, makes even finding a place to sit difficult, nor the hustlers in monk's robes who zeroed in to sell us things. The angry screams of monkeys drifted in the air. They was always quarreling, and it was unpleasant to see the big and strong bite the small and weak, also taking their food. Old sick dogs came to the stupa to die, apparently drawn by the vibrations of the place, poor mangled creatures. In spite of these attacks on eyes, ears, and noses, however, we had the feeling of thoroughly knowing the place and rarely left before dark, even though Kathmandu was full of exciting friends.

The great Joy-Buddha statue inside the temple radiated great power. Often we felt it was actually breathing, and the music of the red-robed monks was spellbinding. We did not understand its inner and secret meaning until much later, but that was not necessary to experience its power.

During the first visits to Swayambhu, two monks made a strong impression on us. One of them was Sabchu Rinpoche, later our teacher of "peaceful" and "wrathful" breathing. He led the monastery and died some years later, showing his realization: it is said that a week after clinical death, he still sat in meditation while the energies in and around him solidified in the form of colored pearls and gems.

We did not know anything then about his accomplishments, but seeing him made us excited and happy. Once, as I spontaneously followed him around the stupa, he suddenly turned and looked into my eyes while saying something in Tibetan, which of course I did not understand. I felt his kindness but at the same time couldn't help cracking up with laughter. At close range he looked like the perfect double of a famous and very amusing Danish sports reporter.

A young monk called Puntsho presented us with a "mala"—the hundred-and-eight strung beads representing the eight levels of consciousness before enlightenment and the hundred Buddha-aspects manifesting afterwards. Then he gave us a small picture of a powerfully built man holding a black crown above his head, saying, again and again, "Karmapa, Karmapa," as if he wanted to impress something very important on us.

At that time an old bomber plane was the means of transportation to Pokhara, the second largest town of Nepal. It lies in a valley to the

The stairs up to Swayambhu in 1985

west of Kathmandu, and the airport was a grassy field. Local transportation consisted of rented horses which we ended up pulling everywhere. In no way would we hit them as the locals did, and without that, they simply did not move. The Swiss had established a large Tibetan refugee camp, which was a joy to see. Here no one had tried to sell the people Western culture or Christianity. Instead, they had been helped to preserve different practical skills, such as weaving, which enabled them to feed their families and themselves. Unfortunately, however, the Swiss were later forced to leave because of pressure from the Chinese, and today the Tibetan refugee camps in Pokhara live mainly from tourism, a much less noble trade.

After some weeks in the country, it became possible to distinguish several different races and cultures, not only individuals. Among the homogenous mass of broad smiling faces first experienced, what attracted us were the ones from Tibet, the country beyond the mountains. We eagerly bought the things they came to sell, understanding each other directly through gestures.

Though their way of organizing their nation doesn't show it, Tibetans are intelligent people. Until well into the twentieth century

Bodhnath, Kathmandu, 1968

they lived like Europe during the Middle Ages: They allowed themselves the variety of a hierarchical and xenophobic central government in the middle and southern part of the country; they were independent but docile nomads in the north and west, and monasteries with separate institutions were everywhere.

All were afraid of the merry Khampa robbers from the east, a warlike tribe that for centuries fought off the Chinese. Among them, everybody was his own king. Thus they truly had government geared to a wide variety of tastes, but this uneven organization is not very important when one meets Tibetans. In spite of a complete absence of democracy, transparency, or Human Rights, a highly developed level of human exchange and an unusual politeness are highly visible. The influence of Buddhism and their sense of humor make most things quite reasonable, and one may feel like having reached a perfect realm. The Eskimo-faced, gentle people of central and western Tibet and the tough, Navaho-looking eastern tribes both have a lightness and inner peace that must come from a meaningful view of the universe.

Materially, many still are among the poorest refugees in the world. Neither claiming racial persecution nor threatening to make war and revolution, until recently they did not arouse much international interest or aid. Also today many children die from dysentery, while most adults have tuberculosis.

Sharma, the host of our fifty-cent-a-day hotel in the center of town, spoke good English. He gave regular up-dates on events in the valley and also supplied the milk-rice and vast amounts of sweet tea that hash-smokers crave. In the next room lived a trader from Kashmir with the typical Indira-Gandhi-features of that region. He was amazed that we sometimes gave his dog a caramel, an unusual gesture in a country where most parents cannot even afford sweets for their children. Claes, who had driven with us up to Kabul, was on especially good terms with him. Claes had flown in with a delay of some weeks. First, it had taken longer to sell his beetle than our VW-bus, and then, on the way through Pakistan, somebody had half bitten his ear off. He had been forced to go to a local hospital, and the stay there had nearly finished him off. Only now was he well enough to come. Perhaps the Kashmiri had heard from Claes how dearly I love my parents and my brother. Anyway, he came to our room one day just as we were off on some very powerful LSD and were therefore very open and easily influenced. He completely won my confidence by saying a lot of wonderful things about my father: what a good man he was. Then he began describing the power of the Lamas who had come to Kashmir from Tibet. He told more fantastic and way-out stories than we had ever heard before, especially about their victories in magic over the Hindu priests. We nearly fell off our chairs from excitement and spontaneous trust. It was amazing to hear firsthand of the miraculous phenomena which were then so important to the West. He said that the following day a lady would visit him who had such powers. If we had some money for her, she would burn butter lamps at holy places in the mountains, and we would be protected from all kinds of obstruction and danger. He also advised us to wear silver bracelets, which would be good for our livers. At that time I had just been through my second bout of hepatitis, Hannah her first. So in saying this he once again struck dead center. Under no circumstances did we want this dehumanizing disease again.

The next evening we started our flight back to Europe as planned. To avoid Indian customs, we had chosen a roundabout but cheaper route via East and West Pakistan. The officials at Indian airports have the nerve to treat Nepal as "inland," and they could have made trouble over the things we had bought. At that time, we imagined ourselves the owners of some valuable ancient Tibetan scrolls and statues. Actually we had made the beginner's mistake of looking more at the patina (due often to a few weeks in a chimney or in the ground somewhere) than at the exactness and quality of the workmanship. Almost nothing we brought back from this first trip, objects judged and chosen with red hash smoker's eyes, hangs in our meditation centers today. Not being accurate representations, they are not able to give enlightening feedback. To truly benefit mind, the right proportions and colors must be used, and the texts describe these very precisely. Only our scrolls and statues of a lady Bodhisattva called Dolkar were always first class. She is the "White Liberatrice" who right from the beginning came to us in so many forms. She showed her power-field after saving my life on a mountainside in South Africa, and in the form of Dukar, or White Umbrella, she now protects my students and myself during fast driving all over the world.

During three amazing weeks, everything had succeeded better than we could have wished, and there was even a pleasant rounding off at the end. The woman the Kashmiri had talked about had come to our hotel. We saw her shortly, had a few words with her, and were impressed by her Buddha eyes and her radiation of deep peace. We gave the Kashmiri twenty dollars in an envelope for her. Claes, whose father had not been praised, had a sharper eye for the Kashmiri than we. He thought I was crazy. He said we should have kept the money for another kilo of the hash waiting in Afghanistan, at half the Nepalese price. Also, at the last moment, the possibility of buying solid silver bracelets against hepatitis turned up. We had thoroughly searched the small shops in Katmandu with no success until someone told us to try the Tibetan Camp. Although there was very little time, a detour was possible on the way to the airport, and within ten minutes, a stately lady brought two 170-gram bracelets of beautifully worked pure silver. She wanted $10 apiece. Touching them, we became aware of something like a light pulse beating in them, a living power. In the years since then we have only come across one at all similar. Needless to say, we left Nepal with the decision to come back.

During a quick landing in Kandahar, we picked up the stash waiting in Ali's hotel. Then we flew on via Teheran to Rome, where we found a drive-away car to deliver in Copenhagen. In twenty hours we reached the Danish border. Here we first did an empty test-crossing, asking if there were any messages for us. It was a relief that there were no complications, in spite of the girl who had talked about us.

Our first stay in Nepal had taken less than a month, but some part of us never left. The experiences had gone very deep and colored our view of life. Although our outer behavior didn't show much change, inwardly we felt that something big had occurred.

Within a few days, Jorgen, a neighbor, fell seriously ill. He lived with a group of us in an old house opposite the embankment of Christianshavn, in picturesque medieval Copenhagen. He fainted on the stairs, looking ghastly with a dark yellow face and red-brown eyes. He had serious hepatitis. I carried him into his flat, and holding him while he peed, his urine was thick and brown. It was his second bout with this debilitating illness, and it was a pity. We had become acquainted in an evenly matched fist-fight years earlier and later developed a close friendship. Motorcycles and drugs were common interests. He boxed, just as I did, and had won most or all of his forty-two matches. As he wanted more energy in the ring than hash smokers usually have, sometimes he improved his stamina with a shot of amphetamine. Apparently he had shared a needle somewhere with someone who was sick, and this was the result. Remembering the Kashmiri's words about our bracelets being good for the liver, I slipped mine over his wrist, then crossed the landing back into our apartment. For a moment, I stopped in front of the shaving mirror on the door and looked into it absent-mindedly. Immediately, an enormous energy hit me, as though I had been plugged into a high-voltage current. I stood like a pillar, a radiant light absorbing all thoughts and experiences. How long it lasted is uncertain, but returning to my senses, I felt burned out and disoriented. All this had happened without chemicals, and yet it was stronger than the experiences I knew from massive doses of acid. Only my first trip in the backyard had been of a similar intensity. I went down to the public baths around the corner, stood for a long time under the streaming water, and thought, "What was that all about? Where did that light come from?"

The next morning Hannah and I went over to Tom's. His face and eyes had their normal color, and he said that his urine was crystal-clear. His night had been full of powerful dreams telling him to stay away from needles. It was a real and perfect miracle! Healing like these just do not happen with infected livers, which require months to regenerate. We were overjoyed. There was only one possible explanation: the bracelets must have real healing powers.

We were still in our room trying to rationalize the event, when there was a knock on the door. Jette, probably the unhappiest being we knew, stood outside. All she said was, "I've got hepatitis!"

Once again we were amazed. We had not seen her for months. She could not have had any idea what had just happened, and yet she had been seemingly drawn to our place. Although she was in very bad shape, wearing Hannah's bracelet cured her in a week. Later she described "lights of grace," which she had seen. She came from the Danish West Coast, where the fishermen live. It is the part of the country that is still strongly Christian, and expressions like that are used there.

Hannah and I were on clouds of happiness. It was an unbelievable joy to be able to help others like that, and further healings continued to occur. In that autumn of 1968 more than twenty of our drug-using friends were completely cured. We often felt the healing energies being activated and also sometimes had unusual thoughts, probably picked up from the mind-streams of those wearing the bracelets. Nothing could now match the intensity of these events, and even our regular trips to Lebanon became rather secondary in their light. We continued more out of habit and because our friends were expecting them of us. All things were geared towards going back to Nepal soon, and on the first day of the winter vacation, when my students would be gone for over a month, we again went east.

CHAPTER TWO

The Transparent Lama

IN ORDER TO COVER OUR TRACKS, this time we went via Russia. It was more time-consuming and expensive but necessary. The train went from Copenhagen via East Berlin to Moscow. From there a flight left via Tashkent and Kabul to Delhi.

East Germany and Russia awakened memories from my time in the army. Then I found self-important officials to be the funniest thing in the world, and now there was more than ever to laugh at. Even stronger, though, was our compassion for the unfortunate people who could not get away from their heavy oppression. Their lives were truly bleak. Unobserved, we managed to distribute the extra nylon shirts, razor blades, and cigarettes we had brought along. It was the best one could do in such a short time.

At Brest-Litovsk, the post-war border between Poland and Russia, once again customs control lasted for several hours. Here something funny happened. I walked through a company of soldiers marching by, probably Cossacks, who looked like me. Some were bigger, most smaller, but we all had very similar faces. Something like this had not even happened in Denmark, and it felt like being in a mirror-cabinet. If I had been wearing one of their brown army coats instead of my own white Swedish one, I could have slipped in unnoticed. It was a dream-like experience and left a notion of how narrow our basis for clinging to a separate "me" really is.

At the Moscow airport, some soldiers came to ask what had really happened in Czechoslovakia. When setting out, their officers had said they would go repel imperialist Western invaders at the Suez Canal.

Having suppressed Slav brothers in a neighboring country instead, they were now thoroughly confused and disillusioned. We told them what we knew, having driven through the country a half-year earlier during the "Spring of Prague," but soon some enormous policemen appeared and dragged them away. They also tried to make the soldiers return our gift of "Senior Service" cigarettes, but we would not take them back. Finally, also the policemen accepted some, hiding them quickly. What a circus it all was!

Two Americans had just landed as the first people on the moon, and our omnipresent "guides," schooled to see everything in terms of East and West, took it personally. "You really won there ... for a change," they said, looking sour. We answered coolly, "That's nothing special. They were up there last year as well, but that time they kept it secret." That didn't improve our popularity any.

We had to stay five days in Tashkent to qualify for our cheap tickets. They gave us some idea of the northern road into Tibet, an experience of the Moslem tribes who now live there, and a taste of the great desert stretching into Changtang, the northern part of Tibet.

Very evident was that Russia is where the white faces go to the Bolshoi Theater or wear the majestic uniforms, while the brown and yellow round-heads build the houses. Where especially the women working in the state apparatus give an impression of deepest frustration, and all things are incredibly shoddy. The wish to open their potential stayed with us until autumn '88, when we founded the first underground Buddhist groups in Petersburg and Tallinn. Now, ten years later, again that vast continent has over 40 centers from Vladivostok to Petersburg, and we spend about two months traveling there every year.

After a flight over impressive mountains—looking like overturned, giant brick-walls—Kabul, Afghanistan, appeared under the radiantly clear, central Asian sky. It was poorer than Tashkent, but a few Western advertisements gave it a more modern feeling. At a constant temperature of about minus ten degrees centigrade, the air was so dry that everything twinkled with its own light. Already then, before the Taleban, the women and poor people of the country suffered a lot.

The vaccination papers needed for India were sold by a gentleman at the Kabul airport. Under no circumstances would any of us even go near the rusty, horse-sized needles on display. We paid a few dollars, and he signed on the right line.

In Delhi we got a two-week visa for Nepal, then for the second time went north by train. We could have flown to Kathmandu on our student-cards; it wasn't expensive, but the tour overland already belonged to the journey. We did not want to just land with a planeload of tourists in this country of our hopes and dreams. Also, the bus ride up is fascinating in winter. We would be able to see the Himalayas clearly, without clouds and rain this time.

Along every step of the way, a longing had grown to see the woman we considered the source of the fantastic healings. We had only chosen the lengthy route through Communist Russia because our file with the police was growing. We should actually have been lying low for a while, but against all better judgment, we had promised to pick up some kilos in Lebanon on the way back, hence our going and coming via different routes. Now that we were nearly there, the necessity for step-by-step planning faded, and we could barely wait to see her again. The bus arrived in Kathmandu in the evening, and we quickly jumped off at the post office. We wanted to avoid the swarms of noisy children at the bus stop who pull at the arrivals and their rucksacks to get them into this or that hotel. This phenomenon had evolved during the past six months, an undignified change which we wanted no part in.

On the way to our hotel in the medieval heart of Kathmandu, we again hungrily absorbed its atmosphere—there were countless adventures to remember and we felt happy to be back. Upon reaching the hotel, people said that Sharma, our source of so much information, was now managing a new lodge near the fire tower. The main reason for our coming was an unconfirmed hope that he would actually know our woman of so many wonders and that it would be possible to build a relationship on a first fleeting contact lasting only a few seconds. So we shouldered our rucksacks and set out once more. Returning via the post office, we bumped into him.

Sharma did know the woman. He laughed at our stories and our eagerness and promised to accompany us the next morning. She was living somewhat outside of town at a place called Maharajgunj, near the waterworks on the street that went by the main embassies. It is an important road in Kathmandu and continues past the Chinese shoe

Hannah with Buddha Laximi

factory. At that time, it here faded into a footpath leading up a hill to the monastery called Nage Gompa at the end of the valley.

The woman lived with her husband's family and a co-wife in a brick house near the street. Behind the house was a well-kept vegetable garden. We heard that her name was Buddha Laximi Lama and took it as a sign that she also had a high official status. We did not yet know that in the areas bordering Tibet the name "Lama" had become a family name, losing its original meaning of "compassionate teacher." We were received by the family and drank tea in one of their low-ceilinged rooms. Then she came in, small, peaceful, and fully resting in herself, with the "meditation eyes" we had not been able to forget. With her brother T. B. Lama translating, we had a lot to say. We thanked her deeply for all the good which had happened, for the healings, and our excellent luck during smuggling trips and fast driving. At that time quite a few motorcycles and used cars were destroyed regularly but never living beings. It was especially wonderful that the protection also reached our friends, and we gave her a golden watch and chain and other gifts we had brought.

Buddha Laximi laughed at our story, and her brother cracked up. She had, of course, never even heard of the twenty dollars we had entrusted to the Kashmiri, and after the short meeting in the hotel corridor, we had not crossed her mind again. She said, "I'm a completely ordinary woman who buys and sells. I have no special abilities, but as you have such confidence, you shall meet my Lama. His power is limitless. Right now he is traveling, but I will arrange a meeting as soon as he returns."

In the meantime, she found our life style much too dangerous. Therefore she would have some "protectors" made for us by a yogi from a Tibetan refugee camp near Mt. Everest. These *sungdue,* as they are called in Tibetan, are objects which are charged with a protective energy. Their power field extends to their wearers, keeping away harm and bringing them benefit. In Tantric Tibetan Buddhism, now called the Diamond Way, complexly knotted strings or folded diagrams tied with threads in the five wisdom colors are mostly used, and they are exceedingly effective. The yogi who was to make ours visited Kathmandu when there was no money in the refugee camp. He made rain for the farmers, and right now he happened to be in the area. She also said that she would sell hash and religious items to us at a low price since we gave so much of it away. Somewhat confused to see our cherished, self-made notions dissolve, and not fully believing her modesty about herself, we said good-bye. We had at least made friends, and her family had had a good laugh. They were glad that such wild people from North Europe would now meet a master of Buddha's teachings.

While waiting for the Lama to return, we again stepped fully into our life with old and new contacts in Kathmandu. Around us things did not look so good. Although we could not recognize it, our vision being blurred by a vast daily consumption of hash, our friends were increasingly freaking out. Many really exciting people who had joined us on the idealistic drug wagon in the early sixties, hoping to create a better world, were then becoming too mad to be funny. Several had already died. Walking space-cases were becoming more the rule than the exception in our formerly so open and happy chemical brotherhood.

Concerning Nepal, however, the outer frame, illusions were less easy to sustain. The wholeness, which we had first found in this small forgotten country, was not only threatened by materialism. Peking exerted a constant political pressure on the government and insisted on building strategic roads here and there. No one liked the idea that China's vast army might one morning roll down these roads and appear on their doorstep. K. S. Lama, a fine man from whom we bought cheap but excellent scrolls and statues this time, passed on information from the few traders who could still travel in Tibet. They were ghastly stories about the total suppression of a both cultural and freedom-loving people.

The objects appearing in the small shops of Kathmandu also told their stories. One day the market was awash with women's well-worn bracelets, a sign that the nomads in Tibet were now no longer allowed to wear such things. As no woman freely renounces these ornaments, which are often handed down through generations, it was not difficult to imagine what situation they were in. Genuine pieces of Tibetan art were cheap and plentiful, and what the museum would not give permission to export during the day, a friendly official would arrive on bicycle and approve for a small fee at night.

Going by mail jeep up the Lhasa road to the hot springs on the Tibetan border, the country across the river felt like a giant wounded animal. The only non-smiling Tibetans we had ever seen were those carrying sacks of barley across the frontier—bridge. Setting them down on the Nepalese side, they returned without even once looking up. It was very strange. These were no longer the Tibetans we knew—those people who still joked as they coughed up blood before dying of tuberculosis.

One woman, who had just escaped by crossing the river, said that they had to quickly hide all Buddhist books and pictures when Chinese came by. People still knew the places where statues, etc., had been hidden, but nobody dared to pick them up. She was very happy to be in Nepal, but like all refugees she suffered deeply over those she had to leave behind.

There was much talk about small incidents at the border (often amusing if one was not personally involved), such as what happened to four Frenchmen. In heavy fog they had mistakenly driven across the unmarked border bridge, were arrested by the Chinese, and not freed until three weeks later, when they knew Chairman Mao's Little Red Book more or less by heart. It was strange to see Chinese who, always in groups and in uniforms, gazed in amazement at the fountain pens and other propaganda merchandise in the shops. They were apparently produced in their own country but could not be bought there. By agreement, the roads and bridges which the Chinese kept right on building should not be able to carry more than a fully loaded truck, but somehow they were always built to carry several tanks.

In the south, Indian politics hit people more directly. Short-sightedly, they rebuffed the Nepalese with stupid minor border-arguments, cutting off all oil when displeased.

Finally the Lama came. He had been journeying to the many monasteries and meditation places under his guidance. Though Bhutanese by birth, up until today his activity keeps Buddhism in Nepal functioning. It is a huge effort as the social structure supporting it is rapidly falling apart. His name, Lopon Chechoo, is widely known and much respected. After spending years with his teachers in Hima-layan caves, he masters all aspects of the teachings. Now we were going to meet him. Buddha Laximi had organized that.

We went to her house as agreed and were first given some very spicy Nepalese food, which we were slowly getting used to. There, as in most of Asia, one eats the same thing twice a day throughout one's whole life. The food in Nepal consists of boiled polished rice, mashed beans or lentils, often potato slices, and maybe also a piece of meat, always with lots of chili pepper. After the meal, Buddha Laximi showed the way to Lama Chechoo, and her brother came along as a translator. In the darkness, we walked through narrow streets and along the paths between rice paddies, surrounded by the sounds of rustling poplar trees. The house was a long, two-story brick building, Nepalese style, separated into two parts. The door in the wall was open, and we went past tall bamboo poles with fluttering prayer flags and into the house. Everything was very simple but clean. Here and there a weak bulb gave off a yellow-brown light, but the greater part of the house was in darkness. Some smiling men and women in red robes (apparently we were in a monastery) led us up a staircase and along a narrow corridor to the Lama's room. As a row of shoes were standing outside, we also took ours off. Then Buddha Laximi stepped in and we followed her.

Finally, we were in the presence of the man whose transmission had been with us in so many different ways, and he looked like all good things combined. He beckoned us to sit in front of him and

The Transparent Lama, Kusho Chechoo

asked from where we came and what we did. As usual I did the talking (Hannah, on her side, frequently does more of the observing), and under his friendly gaze there were no cultural barriers.

I thanked him for the healings through the bracelets and described our trips and exciting, fast-moving lives. It took no genius to recognize that I considered us cool, but he simply took in everything I said. Sometimes he seemed to sink into himself, his eyelids fluttering or half covering his eyes, and he looked as if he might fall asleep, but then again he looked fully present. While sitting there, something happened which took our breath away: The Lama began to dissolve right in front of our eyes. His form became increasingly transparent, and we could clearly see the pattern of the wallpaper through him. When we turned towards the translator sitting to our right and only saw the Lama from the corner of our eyes, he again became solid, but as soon as we looked directly at him, once more he was transparent.

After the old Hindu in Delhi, I had had enough of hypnotic influences. Suddenly, I remembered a trick from the book on Tibetan Yoga we had along. I pulled forth a solid Danish matchbox and held it in my field of vision directly in front of the Lama. Under hypnosis the matchbox should also appear transparent, but it stayed completely solid while I could still see the wallpaper through him. Suddenly overwhelming happiness and confidence arose in me. I felt deeply thankful that the Lama was showing us mind's power so convincingly. He could dissolve his body; it was something he had the freedom to do. I slipped my trusted smuggler's watch off my wrist. It was the Omega model that was first used on the moon, and it had accompanied us on many exciting trips. Sliding it on his arm, I gave my heart with it. Hannah, who so often experiences the same as I, had the same complete openness. Then the Lama bent forward and put his hands on our heads. Thus he gave his blessing, transmitting the power of the Kagyu lineage to us. There was only light; it was a state beyond description. I remember being in front of the Lama's house again, empty of thoughts, and probably with the help of Buddha Laximi, we got a rickshaw and returned to Sharma's hotel.

We did not sleep long. Heavy users of hash are no early risers, but that morning, we were awake at 3 AM. All joy was gone, however. Looking at each other in disbelief, we asked, "Did you dream what I dreamed?" It had been a bad night! Memories of petty and embarrassing happenings had surfaced, mainly from childhood. Stupid lies, meaningless thefts, and worst of all, situations where one had gotten others into trouble—all that could not be transformed and released as interesting stories had come up in unforgettable dreams. We had a most unpleasant feeling that the Lama had walked through our minds, checked them, and found many faults.

The next days were painful. The imprints of the dreams lingered and could not be freed with the understanding we had then. A restlessness stayed, and one day as we were standing in K.S. Lama's shop, an Indian soothsayer came in. He looked in our hands and told us that we would soon lose a lot of money and that in about a month's time, a really difficult period of three to four months would descend upon us. We barely listened to him, however, gave a few coins, and sent him off politely.

Shortly afterwards, a telegram arrived that some friends had been caught after an accident in Lebanon. They were carrying a suitcase full of hash. Now our help was really needed, and it was time to return. Before going, we managed a few defiant actions to make the Indian's bad prophecies come true. Dropping our professional caution, we shelved many good feelings and apparently blocked the powers which protected us. What followed was inevitable.

Until then we had always carried the goods in vests or strapped to our bodies, but now our constant success made us lazy. We had already sent one batch and were again planning to fill larger-than-life brass Buddha heads with hash and export them back to Denmark. As the police were catching and putting away ever more of our traveling colleagues, we wanted to spread ten kilos of the best hash we had ever been able to get, parachuting it in five-gram packages with smoking instructions over central Copenhagen at rush hour. In this way, we hoped to speed up the legalization which always seemed just about to happen—this would be the act to make us all legal and get our friends out of jail.

The hash came from one of the few truly unpleasant men we had met in Nepal, an unusually criminal type. He was the only one who could get us top quality in sufficient amounts. For weighing the stuff, they could only find the meat scale at the butcher-shop around the corner where, in the windows of the room, the last flies were still buzzing after a dose of DDT. Adding to the auspiciousness of the events, Hannah and I were angry and vengeful. We were thinking of defending our friends in trouble as we crammed the hash into the large brass heads. Gurkha-knives, today used mainly for ritual killing, also added to the excellent vibrations of the package, and at the last minute Hannah had the idea to also send some incense sticks. It was clear that their smell would make the customs people jump, and I said so several times, but somehow they were included anyway. None of our hard-earned experience and tricks of the trade seemed useful. Evidently a period of our lives was now finishing and something new would begin.

While preparing to return, we at no time forgot the Lama. As we had never learned to avoid any challenge, we had to see him again. This was quite difficult as he was always very busy, but Buddha Laximi again managed a meeting on the evening we were leaving so we could at least say good-bye. Feeling less cocky this time, we told him both our dreams and how we had interpreted them. He just laughed, however, and gave each of us a small flat package of folded paper with threads in five colors wound in a pattern around them. They were much more accurately made than the kind Buddha Laximi had obtained from the rain-making Lama. Lopon Chechoo Rinpoche said that we would be back within a year, that many things would happen now, and that he would keep us in his wishes; we must never doubt that. His parting words, which we then understood very differently from later, were these: "Everything that happens to you will be good as it is." Small packages of a specially blessed medicine were the last things he put into our hands. During meditation, yogis charge these small, irregular grains of herbs with the energies of different Buddhas. I discovered their strength later, when absent-mindedly eating quite a few of them. The inner energies became so strong that I could not bend my back for hours. They felt like a steel spring in the center of my body.

The Lama blessed us one last time, and we left touched and thankful. Buddha Laximi's parting present was a mantra: a series of syllables to stay in contact with him. Eagerly memorizing them, we drove to the airport.

CHAPTER THREE

Freedom in Jail

STOPPING IN LEBANON AS PLANNED was not advisable anymore. It was certain the police had our names by now, and we also had to get back as quickly as possible to reassure our parents and help our friends. At the last transit-stop in Frankfurt, we called and learned that the first box with Buddha-heads had already arrived. Now the question was getting ourselves into Denmark.

Being in a hurry, we flew straight to Copenhagen, trusting as always that our luck would hold. At the airport we repeated our mantra and fell in behind two policemen leading a pair of arrested Greenlanders through passport control and customs. The officials thought we were also police and let us through without checking.

Our dear parents were not happy at all. They did not share our conviction that we were liberty fighters for the noble cause of inner freedom, helping people to get rid of aggressions and alcohol. They saw that their children were in big trouble: some papers already stated what the police suspected us of doing but could not prove.

We had not been back long when the second box arrived and was seized by customs. Smelling the incense had made them suspicious. They opened the heads and found the hash we had intended to spread over Copenhagen. The package had not been addressed to us, nor had it been sent by us, so we were in the clear. The heat was increasing, however, and we felt the protective wall around our work crumbling. Ever more friends were rounded up, and at the same time, our protectors seemed to have disappeared. We could not find them anywhere. A further warning came in a snowstorm near our house in the Swedish woods—we got a ticket for speeding, which had never happened before. Barely had we brought our most valuable possessions to the houses of friends before the police arrived.

We could have disappeared in Southern Europe until the heat wore off. There was a clear meaning to the signs, however, and what was unfolding must be something we should learn from. Had we not been told many things in advance, and had the Lama not promised us his protection, no matter what happened? We knew that events were at least influenced by him, so we let cause and effect rule.

The police had worked hard. They had gathered all kinds of loose ends together and had enough to hold us. It was just the time in Denmark when they wanted to change smuggling from a petty offense into criminal act, and in order to do so, they needed colorful test cases and much publicity. In a small country like ours, with high taxes and a long coastline, smuggling is traditional, and we had always thought of our activity as an exciting gentleman's sport. In the meantime, however, foreigners had entered the trade with methods which were not so gentlemanly. Moreover, the really damaging drugs, such as opium derivatives, were arriving in ever bigger quantities. They were now being used by people from weak levels of society who had no alternative. Apparently the noble phase of mind expansion was over, and the government obviously had a reason for wanting to put an end to it.

Although Hannah and I had always lived as cheaply as possible, equating thrift with freedom, the police could still prove that we had spent more on cars and travel (then as now our only real expenses) than I could have earned with my teaching job. The question was only how much to admit to. We had to cooperate to some extent; otherwise the highly pregnant woman who had received the second box would have to give birth in jail. Also, I wanted to get Hannah out as soon as possible—small rooms with no handles on the inside of the door were not exactly to her taste. So I decided to admit to what they could already prove. I claimed Hannah had known little or nothing about my transactions. And with regard to others, I only knew an Arab by the name of Joe. I repeated this story at every grilling, telling the police that I would under no circumstances grass on friends. The two policemen who interrogated me didn't like it, but having been in the Resistance movement during World War II, they very well understood my position. I knew, however, that I must get the case to court as quickly as possible. If they got the information from the Middle East they had sent for, we would be in major trouble. I absolutely had to make our case an emergency.

So, on a fine morning, I put a knife into my chest, slowly and consciously, leading it along my ribs in order not to destroy too much. The pain was not too bad; most unpleasant was the noise with which the muscles loosened themselves from the ribs. But with the knife up to the handle in my chest, it looked dramatic enough, and the authorities really thought that I that tried to kill myself. I was put into the hospital jail, and the trial was speeded up.

Although we only met once during this time, Hannah and I were in constant contact. In daily letters, we noted the hour when things came up in our minds and it mostly corresponded. The police, who read the mail, soon gave up trying to play us off against each other, and a well-known psychologist, to whom we later gave the letters, had never seen anything similar.

Very typically, my first meditation experience occurred while teaching someone else. My companion in the hospital room was a poor fellow, who, though clearly disturbed, had somehow not come under the broad wings of the state. Instead he had become a freelance burglar and here reached a high level of skill. The story of his life was without direction, and I couldn't help feeling compassion for his frustrated, roving state of mind.

One day I heard myself saying to him, "What you need is meditation." Though I only knew the subject from reading the Tibetan book, I at least wanted to show him what it looked like. Sitting up in the straight posture I knew from pictures and Buddha statues, I got much more than expected. Hardly were my body and legs in position, when something amazing happened: everything became radiant and I felt like floating in the air—there was no feeling of a body any more. Behind my forehead, a sweet kind of pressure was building up, as if a fine wind was moving underneath my skull. The Lama, Hannah, my parents, and friends—everything good—was very present, and there was great joy. Hannah felt this great opening strongly, and in her next letter she asked, "What did you do that time? It must have been something really good." From then on, we both meditated several hours every day.

By the time I returned to my solitary cell, I had decided that we were invited by the state to learn meditation, and from then on we hardly did anything else. It was very blissful, also the pressure inside our heads, which moved between our foreheads and the top of our skulls. Due to its power, for a while I suspected having contracted some kind of disease in Nepal, but the feeling seemed so "right" that I did not want to involve anyone in it. Somehow, also this had to do with our Lama, and what could one tell a doctor about inner experiences, anyway? I preferred taking the risk of having some disease to losing the wonderful feeling of total unity.

In the meantime, the police had found our protectors, and one night I experienced the power of these diagrams.

I have always managed to have an exciting life. Already as a child, the tallest trees were not tall enough, and later the fastest motorbikes were not fast enough; fear and anxiety are feelings I never really knew. Where others stand back from danger, permitting fear and separation to manifest, I leap right into what happens and experience much joy in doing so. One night, in the cell, however, I awoke with a pressure in my heart that must have been fear, real fear. I felt that it had to do with the protector around my neck, so I put it on the shelf above my bunk. The feeling around my heart left, and I slept on. The cells were completely dark at night—we had skilled servants for even the simplest things, such as turning on and off the lights—but the next morning it became apparent what had happened: one of the threads around the diagram had become untied, changing its form. I returned it to its original shape, and since then I have been extra aware of the physical state of my protectors. It is wise to keep that type inside a bag.

On the same occasion, copies of *Tibetan Yoga and Secret Doctrines*, which had been along on our last trip, were brought to us, and this was the time to focus on their content. Connected through daily letters, we worked our way through page after page of advanced meditations and shared wonderful experiences. With more luck than wisdom and a frequent feeling of already knowing the practices, we successfully used very advanced methods, techniques which actually require the initiation of an authorized teacher and years of preparation.

After my feigned suicide, things speeded up, and in six weeks, our case came before a judge. The name of the judge was "White," which we considered a good sign. I gave my explanation as if in a trance, heard my own voice speak, and at the same time had the feeling that it was not me talking. I told them how much we believed in the expansion of consciousness and that hash had helped us become less aggressive and more open to others. I also told them about the healings and the Lama in Nepal. Drugs, healings, the liberation of mind! At that time we mixed them all together and thought that where the fruits were so good, the tree must be excellent. We did not see that there were very different fruits and trees in this game. The main investigators had gradually swung to our side. In the court, unusual feelings of sympathy spread, and in the end, even the D.A. defended us. We got the lightest sentence possible in this case: Hannah was able to go at once, and I had to do four months. With the time in custody included, I would be free on mid-summer's day.

People higher up in the police, however, were not amused. They knew that we had made things difficult for them for many years. Alone or with friends, we had done our utmost to disturb their work and help those in trouble. We had covered people's trails, helped comrades and goods to safety, and taken private revenge on policemen who went too far. There was much anger about the mild sentence, and they immediately appealed. It was clear that they wanted blood and that by this time they would probably have new, more incriminating evidence from the Middle East. It looked like real trouble. On top of that, the higher courts were booked up, and no appeal was possible until September. It was now the beginning of April, and they wanted to keep me until then.

Hannah fell sick at the news and I burned with anger. We now focused on two possibilities: either the Lama would help us as he had just done (though we had no idea how), or we would attempt the last meditation in the book. It is the transference of consciousness called Phowa in Tibetan, by which a practitioner's mind can consciously leave his body.

Practices of this kind are known to the Diamond Way. One of these, a Phowa called Dronjug, was a favorite method of the great Tibetan yogi, Marpa. It permits the transmission of mind from one body to another. Many had used the teaching for practical jokes, however, so it had been allowed to die out. In our first quick glance through the meditations given in the book, we had missed its true aim. We thought it would enable us to leave our bodies in a state of hibernation during the time in jail, while our minds moved around together freely. This teaching, however, is for going to a "Pure Land." It deals with the much more important transference of consciousness at the moment of physical death.

Readers of this book might well ask how we could believe in such things—after having spent so much time at fine universities and even teaching practical subjects like philosophy and languages. Due to our experiences, however, Hannah and I fully shared the views of our "hip" generation. We were convinced that the only borders to mind are those of ignorance and habitual thought—that its true nature is unlimited. This was to become an unshakable certainty during the coming years. Also, what was then very much theory would fully pale compared to the work which followed.

In our dilemma we wrote to Lama Chechoo, telling him what was happening, and three weeks after the court case something happened which is probably unique in the history of Danish justice. For no given reason, the state's appeal was canceled.

The General Prosecutor and the people from the drug squad were exceedingly angry, saying that someone must have lost his mind in the Ministry of Justice, accidentally withdrawing their appeal. It is a fact, however, that at this time Lama Chechoo closed himself up in his room in Nepal for five days. Here he did a kind of dream meditation in which the mind leaves the body in the form of a chosen Buddha and can travel anywhere. Is it any wonder that we love him so much?

After three exciting months of solitary confinement, the last few weeks were spent among other inmates and were not eventful. It was a time for observing the lives of fighters, frauds, and drunks, and compassion was automatic. They clung very much to things as being real, making suffering very real at the same time.

My release was celebrated with a great feast on mid-summer's day. Hannah and I were overjoyed to be together again and so were our friends and especially our wonderful parents. We decided to never again risk forced separations, knowing that this meant the end of smuggling.

At that time I might actually have drawn some conclusions from frequent experiences during the last months. Visiting friends had often slipped me pieces of hash. Smoking them later in my cell, however, brought the surprising discovery that they didn't benefit my meditation at all. Actually they made it weaker and more superficial. Timeless peace, concentration, and joy all would disappear with the first puff, while confused thoughts crowded in. It felt as if all good spirits had suddenly left. During the weeks of celebrations after my release, however, this understanding disappeared under clouds of social smoke. Once again we were guides on the old drug scene.

Fortunately, our connection to Lama Chechoo could not be lost, in any state of mind. The sweet meditational pressure was constantly there, promising to open up further dimensions at any moment. Everything had a many-leveled, expanding meaning. Our world was whole and we felt growth. After some months, the sign came for which we had been waiting. Red-haired Alan, our buddy also from mountain climbing in Scotland, came to Denmark. His American friend Bill wanted a used VW bus to go to Nepal. We bought it, packed our rucksacks, and went along.

CHAPTER FOUR

Overland to Nepal

IN THE WARM COUNTRIES ALONG THE WAY, few things had changed. The Turks drove and behaved below description and parked their trucks at night without lights, preferably in the middle of the roads. Every few miles was another total wreck. We drove in the same style, even teaching them a few things. The Turkish food was healthy, with lots of proteins, but the further east one went, the more suppressed and violent were the adults, while the shorn-headed kids with old faces threw stones at the car. The men were sitting around idly and in droves, always wearing caps, nursing glasses of sweet but bitter tea. They were clearly frustrated, and women were nowhere to be seen.

Iran had become richer. During our first travels through this country, cars barely survived the washboard of the central road. Now, however, the northern road past the Caspian Sea was nearly finished. It was pleasant to drive on asphalt, but otherwise there was nothing uplifting in that country, especially not the people. We frequently had to force them to be at least somewhat civilized towards each other.

Afghanistan was again the oasis on the way, the place to renew faith in humanity. There was no Taleban then, and one felt right with the calm, self-contained people. They somehow belonged where they were and did not need to play games. One had the feeling of an intact culture, where at least the men were satisfied with the values and had no hurry to exchange them for the uncertain liberties of a modern world. One could still feel the vastness of the desert in them. However, there were already more youngsters working as hustlers, and ever more frequently one heard the dreaded, "Hey, Mister!" It was like Morocco in the early sixties, where year by year I had watched the weakening and commercialization of another formerly self-contained people. In Afghanistan it had not gone that far yet; the locals were still honorable. Until one needed to contact them, one was left in peace; one was still a guest and not their prey. They did not stick to one's heels as in Turkey and Iran, nor did they stare constantly at the Western girls, so totally different from their own tent-like, mummified women.

Herat, the first real town in Afghanistan, held lots of funny memories. There the real "East" started for us. In 1966 three Danes, "Harald the Prophet," Anders, and I, had climbed the walls of the castle between the new and old town, freaking out some soldiers who guarded what seemed to be the oldest cannon in the world. Harald now followed a Hindu teacher, and Anders, who had not stopped taking drugs, had died on a dunghill in Karachi shortly after. Nobody knew of what, maybe from untreated dysentery. He was very paranoid when we last met and imagined evil gypsy queens everywhere. The drugs had really wiped him out.

A walking tent in Afghanistan

Very little had changed since our first drive east, where we had brought along Christian with the broken back. He had already been in Afghanistan in the early sixties, as well as helping to open the trail to Morocco some years earlier. Because he regularly volunteered to smoke hash for the dead (a custom among some of the tribes), frequently towards evening he ran naked in the streets. Therefore he knew several jails between Herat and Kabul from the inside. Also Karachi prison had hosted him some time. Here he was beaten daily by the wardens and contracted hepatitis. The jump from a window, which crippled him, happened when, on acid, he suddenly thought that his liver had burst. He then wanted to end it all as quickly as possible. In Kandahar, Kabul, and in the towns on the road between, the police, old acquaintances of his, had come several times to ask, "Hello, Mister Christian, how is your mind now?"

In Herat we again found the small hotels with the bed bugs that shared my good taste in especially enjoying Hannah, and the taps from which no water ever ran. Also the Afghan Cola factory was still in the back room. Afghan Cola is a poisonous green or violet concoction that is sold in used Coca-Cola bottles. A few swigs are enough to bring a European to the toilet in ten minutes, only to find a long line eagerly waiting, and from there to the nearest dispensary in order to buy antibiotics. The drugstores there healed much more than diarrhea. The best German morphine could be picked up without a prescription, and the pharmacists were amazed how many young foreigners needed exactly this medicine. Being born traders, they quickly learned to increase the price to what the market would bear. The local hash was of the "knockout" kind. It was soft, dark green, and very different from the Lebanese and Nepalese varieties. It came from the north, near the Russian border and frequently froze whole parties into immobility. At harvest time, the peasants run through the fields in big suede coats, and the sticky resin they scratch off them is highest quality. It was then selling for fifteen dollars a kilo.

Safe for every stomach were the big sheets of bread, good every-where, and their minuscule eggs. Also, the yogurt is not bad, after one lets the water run off. The yogurt culture is said to kill tuberculosis, which destroys most of the local cows. For health, however, one should mainly stay with local bread and, of course, the black tea, which is sold everywhere. It comes in pots that have been mended till they are pieces of mosaic art. At less than two cents a cup, it speeds one from place to place even during the worst heat of the day.

The southwestern road from Herat was made by Russians, and it was hardly ever used. Sometimes one saw an old school-bus, donated by the USA, with people and animals nearly falling out of the windows, or a car belonging to an Indian or Pakistani who had earned money in England and was now going home. Sometimes one had to stop while a herd of camels was crossing the road, taking their time. Otherwise, however, one was alone with the desert and its many colors.

In Ali's hotel in Kandahar, we again met Danish friends. Here we had often celebrated for days, and the hotel was still the hip meeting place there. Ali now had an additional hotel, but his brother was sulking in the corners. He had just bought a new wife for about a thousand dollars, and now she didn't want to make love. Some had just seen the remains of Eik, a legendary singer and text-writer. We had partied here together the year before. In October '67, he had brought the use of hydrobromides, medically known as Romilar, to Denmark, thus initiating a magical autumn with much collective consciousness. Now, unable to cross the border into India from Pakistan, he had killed himself with an overdose. His parting note said, "I have done this all by myself; nobody is at fault but the negative force in me." Among his last visual impressions may have been a picture of Buddha, which made us glad. We knew that it helps one attain a good rebirth.

This time we wanted to try the southern route into Pakistan via Quetta. The way through Kabul and the Khyber Pass was already familiar. As we got closer to the Pakistani border, the idea came up to celebrate the memory of Eik in the style of our last meeting: with a shot of the good morphine that they sold. Actually I was not much turned on by the thought. After two cases of hepatitis, which I had brought on myself in Morocco and London in the early and middle sixties, I had some mixed feelings about the subject. The last time I had been offered a shot in Denmark, a country completely without earthquakes, a bookshelf had loosened itself from the wall and, against all laws of nature, made a trajectory across the room, landing with a corner directly on my head. Although I had a fishy feeling also this time, it was not possible to say "no" and spoil the fun. No flash appeared as in the old days, only a feeling of heaviness. I felt that my protectors were not pleased and decided to be careful.

Shortly before the Pakistani border, stand some strange mountains that Bill and Alan wanted to climb. They look like piles of big stones, and I have only seen similar formations in Rhodesia. For once I did not try to arrive first by the most difficult route but kept back, bracing for something unpleasant to happen. And so it did. Bill, who was climbing above, loosened a big stone with his foot. I saw the rock in slow motion, pressing myself against the face of the mountain, but it hit my calf. Until Delhi I could hardly walk, and the pain and blood were good teachers. This was the last shot of my life.

The southern way through Pakistan was rough. From Turkey and on, the locals quickly make the round potholes square, and then apparently leave them. The trucks and buses try to run one off the road, and one has to use any trick to get through. The tall, European-type men are walking fortresses, with homemade rifles, pistols, swords, and cartridges hanging everywhere, and the few women hushing by are dressed in tents. They glance furtively into the world through meshes in the material. The weapons we saw were stamped with "Made in Germany," often with the "G" pointing the wrong way or standing on its head, and they appeared as dangerous to be behind as in front of.

In Lahore, it took a few hours to get the permit for the last part of the road towards India. The officials there are quite a show, running around in shorts and with starched plumes standing upright on their hats. Here, as elsewhere in their colonies, the English must have had a giant laugh putting their natives into opera costumes; if it was not done as a joke, then surely it was mean to dress them up like that.

On the Indian side of the border, the customs people had installed a lady with reputed psychic powers who was feared by all along the route. With insistent sweetness she confiscated the illegal rupees and other smuggled goods people brought with them. We raw men, receptive to her charms, gave her a small piece of hash. We could have left Hannah to deal with her but expected it would sidetrack her from the illegal money we were taking in.

In India nothing had changed. The paranoia following the laws of emergency which were imposed at that period had not struck yet, and people were exceedingly noisy but friendly. It was a good feeling after the Moslem countries, where we had to push people away at every stop. From Istanbul on, the masses often wreck peoples' cars in mute frustration as their excitement builds up. Not even India, however, is advisable to visit by car if it is not absolutely necessary, e.g., for transporting lots of equipment.

Gas is expensive. One becomes a showpiece and yet at the same time is separated from the population. Using the rickety, overfilled, late-running buses and trains is more maturing. Here one experiences many of the "human" situations which Western institutions hide away. Also, if one leaves a car at a place where people have access to tools, upon returning one often finds only the outer shell. The borders are especially famous for this. As one is then looking over the remnants, a couple of friendly people—often from the police—will quietly appear and say, "We do happen to have an engine and some tires and headlights which might fit." Then you can buy half your car back again.

In Delhi we got the visas for Nepal quickly, but Bill had something to do there, so we stayed a few more days. We used them to visit old friends, early dropouts from the Copenhagen drug scene, who now lived there as disciples of a Hindu swami. He was the first to become known and establish a Yoga school in Denmark, and we wanted to check him out and see what he taught. As already mentioned, Hannah and I never felt attracted to the Hindus. They are too sweet, controlling, and personal for us, and this Guru in particular was far out. His claim that celibacy was the only way to liberation was nonsense to Hannah and me. How could something, which so unites beings in joy, transcendence, and limitlessness be bad? We knew that Tibetan meditations contain methods for uniting space and bliss. They use the intensity of sexual union as a means to quick enlightenment, so in this central teaching, the guru would not find any takers.

As the Swami entered the room, however, and began to teach the segregated groups of white-dressed men and women, he left out celibacy. His subject was healing, which was so very important to us. We were still deeply thankful for the wonders which had taken place; they had opened a whole new world to us. The Swami had other ideas. He said one would go crazy healing others and that one should let people carry their own karma. As proof he gave several examples from his own experience and even mentioned the names of known healers from Copenhagen now residing in mental institutions.

As the word "karma" comes up in this book often and is not well understood in the West, here a short explanation. To an enlightened mind it is the free play of space, and to ordinary beings it is the chain of cause and effect. It binds them due to their ignorance, and it rules the conditioned world. The karma experienced is the accumulated subconscious impressions of this and countless former lives. If not purified or transformed, the impressions will mature by their own power. Bringing inner and outer conditions together, they cause whatever happens now, at death, and in future lives. Like a strong dream, both personal and collective, karma binds beings tightly when they do negative things, and loosens its hold as one acts from the feelings of oneness with others. However, the law does not fully fall away until the empty, clear, limitless nature of mind is recognized at enlightenment. With the methods of "Great Way" or Mahayana Buddhism, beings of great compassion can absorb and change the negative karma of others. They not only remove the effect, suffering, but also its ultimate cause—the ignorance which causes one to see separation instead of unity.

The Great Stupa at Bodh Gaya

The Buddha in Bodh Gaya

We did not know this at the time, so hearing the Swami disturbed us deeply. We knew he was a wise man, so I jumped to my feet and said, "If it is the karma of others to be sick, then it is my karma to help them. You are a cold fish." The Swami just laughed and said, "Now sit for meditation." An hour of focused concentration followed. We met him later, also in a good atmosphere but politely avoided any exchange of views. We were just too different. As we wanted certainty about the healing, however, we later asked our Lama. His answer was, "Do whatever you can to benefit others and don't think about yourselves." That was a teaching we could understand. It fit simple minds.

To our surprise, Bill, who manifested the least need in our group for a cohesive view of the world, insisted on going to Bodh Gaya. We were not thrilled with the idea. On the map, Bodh Gaya was well off the direct route to Nepal, along bad roads. Hannah and I only wanted to meet Lama Chechoo, while Alan had seen enough Indians for a while. It was Bill's car, however, and he was our friend. That decided it. We had hardly even heard of the place, but arriving there we learned more.

Bodh Gaya lies in the vicinity of Gaya, in the province of Bihar. It is the place in Northeastern India where the historical Buddha manifested his enlightenment. Actually, it is said that this powerfully charged place is where all the Buddhas who start periods of enlightening, beyond-dual teachings, go to finalize their realization. Prior to Buddha Sakyamuni, who taught during 45 years about 2550 years ago, three other Buddhas had appeared on this earth. In all, a full one thousand will manifest, liberating countless beings until the end of this world cycle.

All the different schools of Buddhism have temples at Bodh Gaya, and although our thoughts never left Lama Chechoo and Nepal, we were still amazed at the many faces of it all. Of course, even in Bodh Gaya we felt drawn to the Tibetans. We had the good fortune to meet the new incarnation of the Dukpa Lama, who in his former life had been the teacher of Lama Chechoo, and received a strong blessing from him. Also two Lamas were there who would later have much activity in the West: the Thubten Yeshe and Thubten Zopa Rinpoches. As the former was a nun in his last life, he understood women very well. Arriving at the Tibetan monastery, Ling Rinpoche, one of the two main teachers of the present fourteenth Dalai Lama, was just giving an initiation, which we walked right into. Here we were each given a rupee, which touched and embarrassed us, coming from such poor people. We also received a piece of meat, which, as year-long vegetarians, turned us off. In our ignorance we quickly gave the rupee to a beggar and the meat to a dog. Today we know that one should eat at least a little of, and mentally accept, what is given during an initiation. However, we still felt that we got a blessing. After three days of counting the hours, we finally drove on to Nepal.

CHAPTER FIVE

The Black Crown

O N DECEMBER 22, 1969, we reached Kathmandu. Rattling our VW bus into town, we were amazed to see dozens of old friends standing along New Road. They called out to us, "Karmapa is here! Karmapa is here!" We had arrived in Nepal minutes after Karmapa, the greatest meditation master and first incarnate yogi of Tibet. For the first time in thirteen years he had come to a place where Westerners could meet him.

Since 1110 A.D., Karmapa has been Tibet's first consciously reborn Lama and recognizes himself at each new birth. He also finds incarnations for other Tibetan lineages, and the first Dalai Lama was a student of a student of the fourth Karmapa. Since fleeing Tibet in 1959 with hundreds of his people, taking them through the Chinese lines and the Highest Himalayan passes without casualties, Karmapa had busily founded centers of meditation in Sikkim and Bhutan, countries which at that time were closed to foreigners. Now, for the first time in many years, here was the chance to see him. Not until later would we realize how events had been falling into place for a long time and on many levels. They were now perfect for activating our bond with Karmapa, which went back many lifetimes. My strong recurring dreams since earliest childhood of protecting the lives of lay people and monks, while fighting back hordes of Chinese soldiers among jagged mountains, would now make sense, as would Hannah's spontaneous Tibetan-style singing and dancing from her earliest years.

First eye contact with H.H. the Karmapa on Swayambhu

At that time, however, we were not so open to these signs of battle and beauty from former lives. We were looking for Lama Chechoo only and were interested in nothing else. Several times a day we drove to his house in Maharajgunj and each time heard the same: he was with Karmapa. We had a lot to tell him and wanted to thank him so very much, but as there was no possibility of visiting him privately, we decided to go to the Swayambhu Stupa. This was where Karmapa was staying and therefore, also Lama Chechoo.

As we came to the foot of the mountain, it was clear that something special was happening at its top. More Tibetans than we had ever seen at one time were standing at the stairs wearing their best traditional clothes. They were gazing upwards, happy and excited. Holding their hands together at their chests, they expressed thanks and devotion. Down the sides of the hill rolled the deep growl of the long Tibetan horns, and their vibrations filled the area. Suddenly, everybody started moving up the steep steps past the large, freshly painted Buddha statues to the temple at the top. We also felt drawn there, and I took Hannah by the hand, running up the stairs past the more slowly climbing locals. As we arrived at the stupa with the *dorje,* the expression of Diamond-like Enlightenment marking the top of the steps, the horns changed to an oboe-like shriek. To the right in the yard was a compressed mass of Tibetans, all looking intensely into the opening of the monastery. In the semi-darkness, inside the doorway, sat a powerfully built man in red and yellow on a box-like seat. He was holding something black above his head. At first, in the glare of the sun, we could hardly see what it was. After a few minutes, he lowered it and placed it in a kind of box while the iron-gate was quickly pulled shut in front of the opening. For a moment everyone stood as if struck by lightning; then they began to move. All forced their way towards a small side door in a niche on the left, apparently trying to get to the man on the throne. There was an incredible pushing and squeezing, children started screaming, and suddenly I found myself in the role, which later so often became mine among Tibetans, of holding the strong and young back in order to let the old people and children in first, protecting those who easily get trampled in a stampede. One needs a lot of strength for this work, and for the mostly lightweight Nepalese and badly nourished Tibetans it is not easy.

After maybe an hour, the main body of people had passed through. Work was over and we let ourselves be pulled along as some of the last. The stream pushed us along a short, dark corridor, and suddenly, in the blare of the horns, we stood in front of Karmapa. As he put his hands on our heads we looked up, and suddenly he became huge like the whole sky, incredibly vast, golden, and luminous. The people pushed and pulled us on. The unceasing energy made us shake all over, and in a trance we stumbled past red-robed monks putting strings around our necks. Outside in the courtyard again, we clung to the iron-gate in a state beyond thought. We saw only the great golden Buddha in front, blessing the last straggler, and we knew that such perfection one could never forget. The power of Karmapa had entered our lives.

In Karmapa's retinue the best English was spoken by the Bhutanese doctor, Jigme Tsewang. He was a joyful, well-rounded figure, his lips red from constantly chewing betel. He helped us with translations and became our main link to Karmapa. Buddha Laximi also took care of us. Her worry was the dwindling state of our finances. She had noticed that we would never say "no" to charming old

Tibetan ladies wanting to sell us something. Also we were impossible bargainers with people who needed money badly. To save what was possible, she found us a cheap mini-room in the old town with some of her many friends. At least it saved the daily half-dollar for our hotel!

We hardly got our things unpacked. We were at Swayambhu from early morning until late in the evening, leaving only when everyone was asleep. We just had to be close to Karmapa, and he wished to let us know it was okay. Pretty or not, we were his first Western students. After some days, the doctor arranged our first private audience. This was our chance to give him the most auspicious things we had. As signs of the bond we felt, we gave him a powerful, Danish horseshoe magnet and a piece of blotting-paper with one thousand micrograms of purest LSD. Until then it had been our most convincing access to mind's truth and bliss. He looked intently at us for awhile, fed us some sweets, laughed, and had us repeat after him in Tibetan the colors associated with the five Buddha wisdoms. Before leaving, he put his hands on the top of our heads and again gave one of those blessings that never seem to stop.

Late that evening in the clear light of the full moon, the doctor came to give us a small package of folded paper. "There are hairs of all Karmapa incarnations in it," he said. "I didn't think anything like that existed, and His Holiness sends it to you." Excited and touched, we took the small package, and I put it in the left pocket of my army shirt for the way home. While walking, the skin underneath the breast pocket began to get warm, and I felt a stinging sensation in my chest. The pain increased until it felt like something was burning itself into me. I took the package out and put it in my right breast pocket. A burning appeared there too, but it was less intense.

Every night we had the same drama with our hosts in Kathmandu. The house was built before modern locks came to Nepal, and returning late by their standards, the door was always barred from the inside. For some reason I always had to nearly break it before somebody would come to open up, and even more strangely, the family did not seem to mind the commotion. As they could live with it, what could we tourists say? That evening, however, our hosts were awakened twice. When taking off my shirt I yelled out loudly— removing the package with Karmapa's hairs was immensely painful.

The next morning Karmapa gave an initiation at the Stupa of Bodhnath, the largest of its kind in the world. During earlier visits, we had seen only the notorious Chinni Lama there or had been partying with our friends. Now it became evident that there were also several high and incarnate Lamas in the area whom we decided to get to know.

Nobody had announced where Karmapa would be that day; they never did. But we soon learned to join the crowds of Tibetans moving purposefully through the streets. They talked less than usual then and instead repeated mantras, clearly tuning themselves in for something important. Wherever these groups went, that's where Karmapa could be found. With his blessing, some friendly pushing, and mainly because we wanted it so much, we always found places right in front.

This day, Karmapa transmitted the enlightened state of all Buddhas three times. Holding the Black Crown above his head, the power of its form opened deep levels of people's minds. At the same time, the sheer intensity of his concentration bridged our inherent and his realized Buddha minds. This was the meditation he had done at our first meeting, and this method is outstanding even among the many powerful tools used in the Diamond Way. Through the centuries, it brought many to a spontaneous realization of their minds' nature— to enlightenment—and it is one of the main reasons for the transmission-power of the Karma Kagyu School.

During those days in Kathmandu, daily Crown Ceremonies of this kind drew all present to extraordinary levels of awareness and one-pointed insight. Thoroughly mixing his mind with ours, Karmapa planted seeds which would grow in this and all lives until enlightenment.

Each ceremony has different effects, and there is no "set" reaction to expect. My experiences with mind are total and dramatic, peaking through skydiving, motorcycling, love, and formerly with psychedelic drugs, while others may prefer more subtle things. Actually, in spite of its convincing nature, an extreme experience is no better than the more flowing kind that most people have. Like in meditation and love, one should never expect anything when energy is transferred. That effectively blocks one's mind. Whatever manifests then is right, and even no direct experience is okay. The impressions are still planted in the mind, and the results always come, sooner or later. To crack a solid ego like mine, however, dynamite was needed, and Karmapa had any amount. That is why his presence is with us also today and as ever-increasing meaning and bliss. Sometimes during the ceremonies my world exploded into orange lights, and only the Crown was clearly visible. At other times a pillar of energy pushed up through the center of my body, so strongly that I nearly fainted and left me dazed for hours. In two sutras, Buddha himself prophesied that the enlightened impressions from seeing this crown with a real interest can never be lost and will awaken during or shortly after physical death. In that state where mind is no longer bound by sensory impressions, one may fuse inseparably with the crown's energy field. Thus mind will realize its true essence, and one is liberated beyond all dimensions of time and space. At the death of my parents, who were close to Karmapa, as with others who died after attending such meditations, it was amazing how these energies become active. All left their bodies with fine accompanying signs.

Formerly, in Tibet, many high Lamas had only blessed a few people after their ceremonies. In their new common status as refugees, this had changed in a democratic direction, but apparently the information had not filtered down. Therefore, and because some thought that the first blessings are best, people rushed to Karmapa after each Crown Ceremony. There was no jealousy or ill feelings in the stampede, however, though there were many tight moments. While those in front hold back in order not to be crushed, the masses behind only push. All want to get their blessing, and with hundreds and sometimes thousands of people present, things can become quite messy.

In Bodhnath it got especially rough. The multitudes were on the verge of trampling everything, including themselves. For a moment it looked like Karmapa might manifest in a wrathful aspect, taking on one of the angry-looking forms which Buddhas use to protect against negativity. Threatening and surrounded by flames, they are frequently mistaken for demons by outsiders. Then suddenly, a long bamboo pole was in my hands, and I pushed with a previously unknown power, which apparently came from Karmapa. Somehow, I held back hundreds of stampeding people and could channel them to his seat in a trickle. Next morning, my sturdy sandals were deformed, and my body felt as though it had been run over—every inch hurt. Returning to Bodhnath, however, we discovered that something essential had changed.

We were immediately taken upstairs to the balcony of the temple, and several elderly lamas came to ask pointed questions about our background and especially about my strength. They asked for birth-signs and other things we then did not understand, but it was clear that we had now been accepted into Karmapa's inner circle. From then on I was expected to function as his bodyguard or rather, to smooth the waves around him.

Some days later Karmapa went by helicopter to Nage Gompa, a monastery situated halfway up a mountain at the end of the Kathmandu Valley. Here Lama Urgyen Tulku lived with his wife, who is also a Lama (or *Lamini* in Nepalese), and two of his sons. In best yogi-tradition he is reputed to have filled a good part of the valley with his offspring, and some were brought up at Rumtek monastery in Sikkim, which was long Karmapa's main seat outside Tibet. He had it built from 1961 to 1965 at an auspicious location in the eastern Himalayas to provide for people who had fled the Chinese Communists with him.

Hannah and I wanted to be with Karmapa at Nage Gompa as well. We took a bus to the Chinese shoe factory, walked through bamboo groves to the foot of the Shivpuri mountain at the end of the valley, and followed the narrow path up. Hannah soon ran a high fever, a good sign of purification, so I carried both rucksacks. Soon she was so weak that I almost carried her as well.

When we arrived at the plateau with the monastery, Karmapa was giving an initiation. Sitting close and more directly in front than before, we could physically feel his immense concentration while building up the Buddha-energies he was to pass on. He seemed bigger than usual, and we both had the feeling that this was a different Karmapa. We asked Dr. Jigme if this was a thought-form of Karmapa or the real one. He thought it was the real one, but in Karmapa's case, it did not matter much. To make that clear, he told what had happened on the way to Nepal.

In Bombay some politicians had insisted on putting Karmapa through a medical examination. Indians consider Tibetans low caste, and their motivation was not charitable. As the best commandos and

*Sitting outside
with the doctor on
Nage Gonpa*

only paratroopers in their army are Tibetan and would completely
follow the high Lamas, they want to know how long the incarnations
may last.

Karmapa had other things to do but could not really say "no" in
the country which hosted so many Tibetan refugees. The results of the
examination were startling. The x-rays showed alarmingly large lungs
and a heart the size of a walnut. In his urine they found sugar and in
his saliva typhoid. The authorities could not believe it, and when he
landed in Calcutta a few days later, they insisted on a second check.
This time the x-ray showed a heart the size of a football with very thin
lungs around it. Instead of typhoid, they found cholera, and the sugar
was gone.

A few days before Nage Gompa, Karmapa had accepted an
examination offered by a German doctor named Fischer. For years,
the doctor had done excellent work for the poor people in Kathmandu, and it was a true offering. On this occasion Karmapa's heart,
urine, and saliva were normal.

While the doctor's words so absorbed us that we hardly noticed
the splendid view of the valley, a line of young girls started up the stairs
into the upper part of the building. They walked with their heads
down, and each carried a white scarf in their hands. Apparently,
Karmapa was again seeing people so we quickly entered the procession
and slipped into the room behind them. When Karmapa saw us, he
roared with laughter. He was ordaining these girls to be nuns by

cutting a few hairs off their heads, and with me in the nunnery, the girls would have been busy. With a motion of his hand, he invited us to sit next to him, and this was our first occasion to really talk with him for a longer period of time.

He asked us about the country we came from, and I told him about Danes, taking my friends, my brother, and myself as typical exponents for the population. I probably made it sound as if we were still brave Vikings and not the pram-pushing "millimeter democrats" that so many had become. Karmapa laughed and said that he was also tough. He was Khampa, belonging to the warrior tribe of eastern Tibet. While saying that, he punched me on the shoulder a couple of times. Without thinking who he was, I punched him back. He nearly fell off his seat, roaring with laughter. Quite embarrassed, I began to realize what I had just done.

Suddenly he asked, "What do you want from me?"

And I heard myself answer with words which we hardly understood and had no knowledge of having used before. "We want to be Bodhisattvas for the good of all beings."

Our books presented Bodhisattvas as the goal of Great Way or "Mahayana" Buddhism. While moving through levels of increasing insight, they help others whenever possible. This motivation to work for the good of all beings felt completely right. Of all things, we wanted that most.

My answer seemed to please him, and he gave us both a small Buddha impressed in tin. It had a dorje on the other side, the sign of immutable enlightenment. Hanging them around our necks, he said, "It is nothing special, but it's from me."

We wore these pendants until they came apart a few years ago, and one is now in the box I use to transfer his blessing.

The next morning, Lama Chechoo landed in an army helicopter to pick up Karmapa. It was wonderful to see him again. He was always in our minds, and we thanked him for what was happening but saw him all too seldom because he traveled so much. We also had a touch of bad conscience, feeling that we might be weakening our bond to him by so completely following Karmapa everywhere. We still thought in Western "personal" terms and saw ourselves as especially gifted students for whom one Lama would surely envy the other.

Hannah was probably exceptional even then, while I was an aggressive and self-conceited case. A steamroller of undisciplined energy, I habitually flattened whatever got in my way.

Aware of our dilemma, Chechoo Lama repeatedly encouraged us to see Karmapa as our teacher, and gradually our feelings of embarrassment disappeared. Though well trained to think abstractly, there would be frequent disillusionment before we could really learn from life. Understanding first our teachers, and then ever more beings and situations as Karmapa's energy-fields maturing us, took quite some time. It was much easier to theorize about the omnipresent Buddhamind than to accept its power in one's own life.

There was no chance to follow Karmapa to the retreat he would bless that day, so we hiked down the mountain with the others. In Karmapa's entourage were four teenagers, whom we liked immediately. They asked many questions but frequently seemed to know the answers in advance. Dancing from stone to stone down the hillside with them, the few words of English they knew plus the Nepali phrases we had absorbed, supplied the basis for quite a good communication.

Although these young monks were special, the reaction of the mountain people when meeting them surprised us. They quickly took off their hats and bowed while the boys touched their heads in passing. When the sun shines, one does not see the moon and stars. Due to our focus on Karmapa, we had hardly noticed these other four jewels of the Kagyu meditation school.

Though feudal Tibetan society and the condition of having a human body caused blemishes in the lives of nearly all incarnates, these young ones were unusual rebirths. During the last eight hundred years, one or several of them were instrumental in keeping the transmission of the Karma Kagyu lineage between the successive Karmapas. The highest is Shamar Rinpoche, whose rebirths were prohibited by Tibet's "virtuous" or Gelugpa government for 200 years, then follows the Situ, Jamgon Kongtrul, and Gyaltsap Rinpoches.

During this time, many friends from the rough years in Copenhagen came visiting and were blown away by Karmapa's blessing. Although few managed to change much in their lives and would rather take rows of initiations than meditate, still they clearly benefited. Deep inside their minds, a touching confidence arose. It enabled the Buddhas to surround them with a very visible protection.

Around Swayambhu, the valley was feverish. People crowded in from many parts of the world, and Karmapa listened, taught, blessed, healed, and helped day and night. Always there were places where he just had to go and things people wanted. Not once did we hear him say "no" or think of himself.

Among the ceremonies, the "pujas" were very popular with Westerners, especially the ones invoking protectors. Pujas employ musical aids to induce meditation, and the vibrations of the instruments used are sometimes so deep that one's environment seems to sway. The beat of the big drums and the chanting synchronize one's heartbeat and catch one's consciousness. Usually the monks sat in two rows facing each other, holding horns, trumpets, oboe-like instruments, small and big drums, and different kinds of bells. Accompanied by the instruments, they recited texts, which lay on small tables in front of them, concentrating in unison. Quiet passages of recitation were often broken by the loud playing of drums, bells, and horns, and the voices of the monks and lamas sounded as if from another world. Often the experience just floated, and one had no feeling of where the sounds were coming from.

At the end of the row sat Karmapa and the different incarnations on their box-like thrones, all dressed up with yellow robes over their red ones. Much to our surprise, the environment made them neither stiff nor ceremonial. While everything was going on, they chatted, joked, and laughed, looked around, yawned, until a moment came when all were very concentrated. After that, things were easy again.

Whenever possible we brought friends to these pujas. While absorbed in the sound, mental knots opened by themselves. Distant memories came into focus, and ancient feelings arose and faded with the growls of the long horns. Though none of us knew how blessing, initiation, recitation, and so on worked, all were attracted by their wholeness and an energy which one could actually feel.

We knew some of the mantras already, an important part of the recitations. Most of all, we repeated "Karmapa Chenno," which Karmapa had given us himself. Its effect is very broad-spectrum and means: "Activity of all Buddhas, work through me." We felt that it united us with him, made us useful to others, and fulfilled one's wishes very fast. We also did the mantra that Buddha Laximi had given us from Lopon Chechoo Rinpoche, our steady companion while in jail, and of course, the famous "Om Mani Peme Hung," which Tibetans mainly use for the sake of others. This "King of Mantras" is an invocation of Loving Eyes (Chenrezig, Avalo-kiteshvara), the united compassion of all Buddhas, and at the same time, the syllables change six disturbing feelings into wisdom, attach-ment and greed here being of the same basic nature.

> Om – transforms pride and egotism;
> Ma – jealousy and envy;
> Ni – attachment and egotistical wishes;
> Pe – ignorance and confusion;
> Me – greed and avarice; and
> Hung – hate and anger.

Using the mantras confirmed their good effects. Just like the pujas, they stopped inner chatter and gave real peace.

Actually, with a minimum of explanation, nearly all the methods we met with were common sense, useful, and attractive. There was one factor, however, which we couldn't fit in: the much-invoked Mahakala. This name was always chanted when the energy was the strongest, and I knew it was the name of a blue-black power shown on Tibetan scrolls and statues, alone or in union and surrounded by flames. With three bloodshot eyes, fangs, weapons in his two, four, or six hands, chains of severed human heads around his neck, and wearing skins of tigers and elephants, he possesses so many signs of strength and fierceness that one cannot just ignore him.

The energy of these forms always made me clench my fists. Thinking they represented absolute negativity, I would have liked to get my hands on these horrors and thoroughly finish them off. While my Western-conditioned mind held on to this view of Mahakala, at the same time his energy was so familiar that I couldn't keep up my stance. Reluctantly I felt a bond to him grow until a true liking appeared, which I hoped was not a sign of a basic character flaw. I felt I knew nothing better than his forms of raw power, and later on, in addition to the titles of warrior (Khampa) and Dharma-General, Karmapa often called me by his name.

Tibetan New Year is celebrated on the new moon in February or March, and that day Karmapa was to bless both Swayambhu and Bodhnath. Swayambhu would be the site of the traditional Lama dances, and the plan for Bodhnath was a popular feast with local dancers in costumes and masks.

In front of the Swayambhu temple stood a gigantic Mahakala head, and above it was an intricate net of many-colored threads in square and rhombic patterns. During a yearly open-air ceremony, all harmful energies from the past are tied up in the net, and Mahakala, having destroyed and absorbed them, is carried away in procession to a special burning place. Amidst great celebration, evil returns back into space through the element of fire and gives a much-needed clean start to the new year. A group of us were asked to carry the head to the burning-place, and rarely have we toiled as we did going down those steps from the stupa. It was incredibly heavy. When we turned the image over and it was ignited, it felt like victory over everything harmful, and I understood a bit more of what Mahakala is. I realized that he is not negative, but rather the power which conquers negativity, that his limitless energy destroys harmful feelings as well as outer obstacles to our growth. In spite of his exterior, his essence is the compassion of all Buddhas. Today he and his energy-field are the force behind Diamond Way Buddhism around the world.

The Buddhist stupas of Nepal are built to similar patterns, and though increasingly commercialized over the years, the mental focus and bliss one may experience there is mind-boggling. As often as possible, we also meditated in Karmapa's room, and he let us stay there for hours, just absorbing his presence. When we came, he always smiled and said, "Very good."

Meditating on the roof above H.H. Karmapa's head

In his power-field, even those who came to talk about the most important things did not seem to notice the white faces across from him. When the feeling came up that we might be imposing, we walked around on the flat roof of the temple until we felt his upward energy-stream. Placing ourselves directly in it, deep absorption was automatic.

When we were not with Karmapa, we roamed the countryside with friends like Fut, the General, Niels Ebbe, and others from our rough generation, descending noisily upon the countless holy sites which the valley is so full of. After nights of chemically altered consciousness, we circumambulated the great stupas by day. We set the prayer wheels in motion as naturally as do the Tibetans and felt completely at home with it all. Sometimes it was also possible to spend time with Lama Chechoo, to receive his blessing and experience that deep peace which was inseparable from him. After a silversmith at Bodhnath made a tube-like container for Karmapas' hairs, Hannah and I wore it on alternate days. The burning sensation remained where it lay against the skin, and many who held it felt the same.

One beautiful day in spring, Karmapa had to leave. Because people didn't stop coming, he had already postponed his departure several times. That morning, we rose especially early and found our way towards Swayambhu through a fog, which—pea-soup-thick—reached halfway up the hill. Arriving at Karmapa's room via the balcony, to our amazement, Chinni Lama was sitting there. He looked completely dazed, wearing a white coat which Karmapa had just given him. We had the intuition that it referred to cleaning up his act, and by the next day, the purifications of Chinni Lama had already started. Soon much of Nepal was talking about them.

When Karmapa left for the airport, hundreds of people piled onto anything from tractors to trucks and followed him. All were pained by his departure, but while most kept their loss a quiet "inner" thing, it made me unpleasant. There was no logical reason for this. Things had worked out just as we wished. Karmapa had accepted that we should first stay with Lama Chechoo, which due to our high evaluation of ourselves, we had insisted upon. After all, everybody was Karmapa's disciple, while we had only seen few of Lama Chechoo's. Also, we loved life in Nepal and could now stay on. But although Karmapa said that we would soon see him again, the separation felt like an amputation. At the airport, we saw the mental stability of a conscious incarnation. The Tibetan title *Tulku* means "illusory body" and denotes somebody who experiences having but not being his body. Though many children have been chosen as such for political reasons over the centuries, the "real" ones who retain an awareness of mind's nature are often very inspiring teachers. Though rarely officially recognized if not born in Tibetan families, surely many Western idealists merit the title. One of these small tulkus, maybe around school age, had been placed on a table. Standing in the middle of the airport lounge in his red and yellow robes, he was quite a contrast to the noisy kids running around in gray rags. While Karmapa was in a back room with some people from the government, we noticed the strangeness of the situation. Several Tibetans and Nepalese went over to the boy, put down offerings, and were blessed. They seemed happy, but nobody noticed or gave anything to the other kids, which I didn't like. Prompted by a basically democratic feeling, and in order to see what was so special about this child, I walked over to him. With my outer form, large by Tibetan standards, and a five-day-old beard on my face, I loomed over him, grimaced, and loudly said "Boo!" I wanted to see his reaction, but there was none. No fear could be seen, but a clear contact appeared as our eyes met. It was impressive. This child was only pocket-sized, and I pulled Hannah over so we could both receive his blessing. Standing in front of him, he did not put his hand on our heads but instead pressed his forehead against ours. We knew this is a sign of acceptance and recognition, and both felt excellent. With an unexpected light in our heads, we sat down to digest what had just happened. Later we heard that this was the new Ponlop Rinpoche, one of the seven incarnate brothers of the 15th Karmapa and the holder of a high Dzogchen mind transmission.

CHAPTER SIX

The Forgotten Valley

AFTER KARMAPA LEFT, Lama Chechoo again went on one of his
frequent tours. As nothing special was happening in Kathmandu at
that time, we accepted an invitation from our friend Terry Beck. He
wanted to explore a remote valley near Trisuli in northern central
Nepal. Terry worked with the Peace Corps, and a helicopter from the
Birth Control Group had recently discovered this area. A friend of his
had been the first white man to ever enter it, and now we wanted to
have a good look. We knew Terry well from our first visit to
Kathmandu in '69. At that time we had met on a flight to Pokhara in
western Nepal, and he had taught us a lot. He probably knew Nepal
better than anybody at that time, being the only Westerner who had
walked the country for years. His main object was recording local
music, and he had done the full length of the country from west to east
three times, always carrying a full load. Not sparing himself, he never
had difficulties with his porters. As he lived to climb, he had been first
on several of the peaks bordering Tibet. He also took very good
pictures and had collected material for several books, which he
couldn't publish while still in Nepal. Knowing it would disappear
without a trace, he had never deposited the six hundred dollars risk
money with the government for scaling each peak.

There are about thirteen, separate, non-integrating tribes in
Nepal, which all speak different dialects, some being offspring of
Sanskrit and others of Tibetan. Terry knew some of the main Sanskrit
ones and was also a fine organizer. With him and his companion

*The place we parked the Model "A" Ford
before the Forgotten Valley*

Richard, also a trained mountaineer, we would now climb a few "doubtful cases"—passes and peaks which the Nepalese claimed as theirs but which the Chinese insisted were already in Tibet. For that reason, they were strictly off limits.

Our means of transportation came from the Ranas, the caste of immensely rich Hindus who used to govern Nepal. A thousand years ago, when the Moslems sacked northern India, they fled into Nepal with their treasures, soon becoming the governing class. They built the enormous palaces one can still see around Kathmandu. Sometime between the world wars, cars became a status symbol. And so before there were streets in Nepal on which to drive or any gasoline to buy, many acquired the finest on wheels. They were brought by ship to Calcutta, stripped down, and then carried on the backs of kulis over the Himalayan foothills. Now they could be found in the barns of various estates, polished and rust-free. Though often with less than five miles on the odometer, they were sold off very cheaply. Inland transportation had already been taken over by indestructible VW buses—at times we were 23 adults with luggage squeezed into one— or by big diesel Mercedes for the roughest rides, while Japanese imports were used in the towns. The old models were of little use in a country where a quart of gas costs a laborer's daily wage. Thus some of Terry's enterprising friends had bought gigantic, vintage Rolls-Royces, taken them to America, and sold them at a great profit. He and a friend had just bought a brand-new Model A Ford from 1928, which we drove along in.

There were no difficulties on the way, once we got used to such things as the hand-accelerator, and I actually enjoyed driving it. It had an enormous torque. After following the unpaved road to a small hamlet near Trisuli, west of Kathmandu, it came to an absolute stop. From there we would carry our rucksacks. Hannah and I, used to a minimum budget so we can spend more money on Buddha's Teachings, would have gone up the mountain on bread and beans, but our friends had better style. They had bought all kinds of things, which we now had to carry along. To our clothes, boots, kerosene, and sleeping bags, they added all kinds of luxuries, among them heavy jars of peanut butter, special bread, and lots of chocolate. All were available

Making a path through the thicket

Crossing a fast-running river

at the American PX. Each man had more than sixty pounds, while Hannah carried about half.

The first stretch took us along a fast-running river and past a hydroelectric power plant the Russians had built. At the crossing-place, the bridge had fallen down, and there was now a device for hauling travelers across the ravine. Under a suspicious-looking hemp rope, hung a platform with a nice view into the foaming river. Lying on it, one man at a time could be pulled to the other side. It was a relief that none of the rucksacks fell down and that all got well across.

Now some real climbing started, and we understood why so few people visited this valley. In front of us was a rock face which we had to scale, and that brought real excitement. We were later told that here the local women refuse to carry anything and that the men divide up the loads, helping each others while making several trips. We, however, were ignorant of this and just went up individually with our very heavy loads. The view from there to the ridge on the other side became ever more beautiful, with a free drop of a hundred yards straight into the river.

Our rucksacks were built high above our heads to keep the feet mobile and to look bigger than any bears we might meet. However, I had made the beginner's mistake of tying the belt too tightly around my waist. It was hardly possible to hold on to the wall with both hands and feet when the top of the rucksack pushed against the overhang. That gave several good opportunities to internalize the teachings on the preciousness of the human body. After pushing fearless Hannah up ahead and arriving last, our professional climbers said they would never do that stretch again without ropes.

Towards evening we arrived at a U-fork in the valley with a few solid and well-built wooden houses on the far side. The people let us sleep under a projecting roof. As they were Hindus, we were not allowed to enter their houses. We noted that they had the best hash we had ever been near, even in Nepal, and decided to make a contact for them with a friend in Kathmandu. They apparently had no idea what extraordinary quality they had on their hands, and since they were friendly people and kept such a good style with so little, we thought they should earn some money. The next morning, we started up the left fork of the valley. Moving along narrow paths which clung to the mountainside, we climbed hour after hour. Often the bamboo-thicket plants were our height, and one easily got lost. The plants were all brown, and it is said that this bamboo dies every eleven years, at the time when there are many sunspots. Also dead were many of the large juniper trees. When dry, they can split from top to bottom with just an ax, and though the wood is miserably soft, for that reason it is used for the large shingles on Himalayan roofs. In order to maintain a ready supply, the locals dry out the trees by removing a ring of bark around their base, and afterwards much too many stand around, rotting and unused.

Due to overpopulation, Nepal already has massive soil erosion, and the rivers entering India get browner every year. It is a bad sign for the frequently half-starved people in the mountains there.

Late in the afternoon, we passed a projecting rock where the narrow valley turned slightly left. Here lay a half-dozen straw huts clinging to a few square feet of terraced land which did not drop hundreds of yards directly to the river below. Although to our best observation it was impossible to see the path along which we had come, yet the people living there had already made food for us. Most of them had never left the valley and were apparently so united with the area that it had become an extension of their senses. They simply knew that people were on their way.

The men offered to carry our luggage for six rupees a day, then about half a dollar. It was much too expensive for that time, but wanting to be generous, we accepted. In Kathmandu, we had stocked up on brand new one-rupee notes, which mountain-people consider more valuable than the used ones. It diminished the length of the habitual arguments, which to my taste were so demeaning, and we had something nice to give. These people, like already over 80 percent of the Nepalese, were Hindus—they simply multiplied incredibly—and again, we had to sleep outside under a projecting roof. Actually we wanted that. It was much nicer than being inside, no bugs, and we got a good picture of their way of life. It was interesting how they had organized themselves.

The boss here was undoubtedly grandma. She ruled the valley with iron will and a cutting tongue. In order to reach her age in these surroundings, one had to be really tough, and she seemed to have lost

Grandma's village

none of her power. When I took a puff from her water-pipe through my hollowed hands, my curiosity made me cough and nearly vomit. She was smoking untreated tobacco leaves, pure poison.

The porters were small and tough. They set a slow and professional pace without tiring. Their naked feet were nearly square, and softly, like a camel's, they distributed the weight over the uneven ground. Their occasional deep whistling sighs, the signal in the Himalayas that one is under a heavy load, provided a harmonious background sound. It is incredible what a trained kuli can carry, even the skinniest of them, and it is all due to breath control, not muscle. According to gradient, weight, and altitude, they change the relationship between breath and step, and one often has the impression that they consciously change gear. Often they cannot get the cargo onto their backs without help, but once it is there, held by a strap around their foreheads, they can go without stop. Some are even able to carry a heavy Westerner suffering from altitude sickness but only a few miles a day and preferably downhill. On much-traveled routes, there are cabins with hard liquor at the bottom of the steepest rises. They gulp some down and can thus delay feeling the pain of their abused bodies until they reach the pass. Many look like sixty when they are still only thirty years old.

The porters took the three heavy rucksacks, and in order to get into shape more quickly and because I never feel good with others doing the work, I took Hannah's lighter one. These people taught us more than techniques for carrying, they did things we only knew from literature. During the noon-stop, they at once collected dry grass. Then they pulled some loose wool off their open Sherpa-style shirt-jackets, which together with a loincloth was their entire wardrobe. Taking from their pockets a piece of steel with one side polished, they struck this alongside one of the semitransparent stones lying every-where. As sparks hit the wool held on top of the stone, its glow was deftly used to ignite the straw and then some dry wood. Using the varying points of ignition and combustion, they soon had a small fire going, heating the maize porridge which was their lifelong diet. We had marveled at their few dozen plants, standing singly and in small groups near their huts, had been licked by their three-legged, salt-starved cow, and I was still wondering how people could survive on that.

Towards evening we reached an abandoned hut made of branches. It offered a magnificent view down the valley, and we decided to stay there. At first the porters did not dare go near the place. A powerful magician lived there, they said, and it was danger-ous. As we had no accident upon entering, however, they remembered that Hannah and I were usually saying Mantras. They decided our magic might be stronger, and after asking my protection, they came in. They had no mats or blankets along and slept on some bamboo sheets lying around. Turning sometimes one side of their bodies and then the other towards the heat of the fire, they got through the night. It was not an easy life, but we heard no complaints.

The next morning we passed through an area of freshly fallen snow, and although the porters walked barefoot everywhere, they had their minds set on an up-grade: they now wanted to try the tennis shoes which we here exchanged for our trusted army boots. It was a major experience for them, and we let them have it, wishing them so much discomfort that they would be at least somewhat immunized against the world of shoe wearers. Steadily and surely it was moving in on them, bringing immense dangers to their values and self-esteem.

The last pass before the cabin

On the afternoon of the second day, on a beautiful plateau with enormous trees where the vegetation changed, we found a colony of small green plants. They looked a bit like dandelion but had much thicker, low-growing leaves. The porters danced with joy and did not want to go on from there. They only thought of taking the plants home. Known as Datura (Jimson weed), the roots have a strong hallucinogenic effect. During the Middle Ages in Europe, witches used it to induce different kinds of trance, often by smearing it on receptive parts of the body. Also in our times when more elevating substances lacked, the roots were sometimes popular among our friends. They "harvested" them from botanical gardens at night and went on trips, which were free but had more physical side effects than most liked. As with bromides and scopolamine, the long-range effects are harmful to the spine. The porters told us that, by burning these plants, all bad ghosts would go away and that now they wanted to go quickly and cleanse their homes. We thought they might also inhale the smoke but gave them twelve new rupees each and let them run. If they were really quick, they would make it back before darkness fell. After that, even to them, walking would be very dangerous. They promised to put down the shoes at our last stop. We would need them from there on the way down.

Again, we had the full rucksacks on our backs. As we were now four kilometers up, they seemed heavier than before. After a short time, however, we walked like our porters. Letting one's heels touch the ground, even on steep ascents, making very short steps, and moving forward steadily was clearly the way. The only stops were for the frequent pees, which the changes in altitude provoked. Shortly before dark, now another 500 meters up, we reached a plateau offering a breathtaking view. On the right side was Langtang Himal and Gosinkund and on the left, the mountains of Tibet. There were some stupas made by Tibetan travelers and a stone cottage in which to stay. Terry and Richard wanted to map the area the next day and luckily brought their full equipment along, while Hannah and I wanted time for meditation. We climbed a ridge from where we could see both Tibet and the cabin with our packs. In the East one quickly learns to keep an eye on one's things everywhere.

Choosing a seat near one of the rough stone stupas, which like the more orderly, polished kind, symbolize the five kinds of enlightening wisdom, I opened a book on the famous and powerful meditation of "Inner Heat." Though a different version from the one I had used in jail, this was also from the Kagyu Meditation Lineage, which specializes in such methods. Hardly had I started the process of imagination and deep breathing, when the latent energy of mind surged through the center of my body. It was evidently a blessing from a former life. This time around I had neither obtained the teaching nor any other conditions for the practice, which in weaker constitutions may produce a Parkinson-like effect. As all blocks exploded inside me and an indescribable light, energy, and joy pulled me apart, there was no place for questions or doubt.

In this area of the Himalayas, the fully accomplished Milarepa had reached his goal through this very practice. His power today pervades the Kagyu School, and it was his enlightenment energies, unhindered by time and space, which now came to us. Across the valley in Tibet, only a short distance away, lay the monastery of Kyirong. Its principal lama was Chechoo Rinpoche, our first teacher. Close by, he had meditated in caves with Dukpa Lama. During several years he had frequently lived on three spoonfuls of water a day. For the first time I felt a power streaming from my hands and held Hannah closely to pass it on.

In the evening we returned to the stone hut. Terry and Richard were nowhere to be seen. It began snowing, and when we woke in the morning, everything was blanketed by half a meter of the stuff. Although our friends had intended to come back the previous evening, we were sure they would be all right. They had brought the best of down equipment, and the protective energies of the area would surely take good care of them. As night fell once more over the high plateau, our friends finally plodded in.

They were happy about the fire and dove right into the food. They had only encountered a few tight situations. Both kept praising their down outfits and space mats, which had allowed them to sleep comfortably in the snow. Only once, snow-blind, had Richard nearly stepped off a rock and into open space.

Next morning we started on the return journey. The new snow made it impossible to push on. Going down was great fun, as we could slide large distances on our backs. We were also looking forward to getting out of our wet, sponge-like boots soon and into the shoes we had left with the porters. When we came to the place where they should have been, however, the shoes were nowhere to be found. Somewhat displeased, we walked on to the magician's place where they might also have been left and then finally to the cluster of huts where grandmother and her gang were living.

Grandmother did not radiate the deepest of sincerity. She told us that the people with our shoes were somewhere on the other side of the valley, and she did not know when they would be back. Now this sort of irritated us, because evidently this was a ruse to keep them. In the friendliest of ways we informed her that we would wait for an hour while eating, and if the shoes had not arrived by then, we would burn their roofs. When, after an hour, we started taking out our matches (we would, of course, never have burned the possessions of poor people), suddenly the bravest and oldest porter stood there, having just somehow found the shoes. Now again they respected us. They felt they had cheated us earlier by asking too much in wages, and by paying them, we had lost face. This was now all forgotten. They wanted to go on with us to Trisuli and would even carry our luggage without pay. Sometimes we let them have one rucksack, then another, but in the meantime, we had learned how to breathe and now almost enjoyed carrying them ourselves. They had also become much lighter as the food disappeared along the way.

Reaching the place where our roofless model A Ford was waiting, we paid the old man who had guarded it. Then with our three kulis in the open trunk, we drove down the two loops of road bordered by corrugated iron shacks called Trisuli. This was their first visit to a town, and they were so proud of entering it in a car that they insisted we honk the horn so everybody would see them. We did so to the point of embarrassment, helping to write a glorious chapter in the history of their clan.

CHAPTER SEVEN

In the Sherpa Country

WHEN WE RETURNED TO KATHMANDU, Lopon Chechoo had just
come back. It was wonderful to see him, and he had a good laugh at
our adventures. He was soon to leave again, this time for Bhutan, so
there was little to keep us in town. We wanted to go once more into
the Himalayas, but this time not just to climb mountains. The Sherpa
country, which then still possessed a virtually intact Tibetan culture,
attracted us, and if we wanted to go that spring, speed was essential.
Otherwise one might be trapped by the month-long rains of the
monsoon.

Lama Chechoo told us which lamas and monasteries to visit, gave
us his protection, and based upon the many practical experiences of
the last trip where Terry and Richard had been excellent teachers, we
now started out on our own. The best way to get from Kathmandu to
Shercumbu, the "Sherpa Country," is to take the early mail jeep to the
Tibetan border, get off at Lamsango or Barabesi, and then walk
northeast from there.

We arrived in the afternoon. The corrugated iron shacks at the
river were full of Chinese road builders, so we started at once up a
seemingly endless mountain. There was hardly a tree, the sun glowed,
and we had only the water in our canteens. Shortly before dark, which
falls as soon as the sun sets behind the mountains, we found a place
under a roof. They had rice and tea but nothing substantial.

Early the next morning we went on, reaching a nice cool ridge
around noon. After a short, refreshing stretch there, the path again
wound down the mountain-side, and this became the pattern for the

whole week. Up to a pass, down into a valley, and up to the next pass again. A part of the route had stupas, stone-carvings of Buddhas, and other signs of culture. For centuries Tibetans had brought their goods to Kathmandu and India along this path, but soon again we saw only brown, eroded hills and people living in poor huts. From time to time, a Hindu Saddhu begged or a couple of young Westerners gladdened one's eyes with their health and strength. European faces were then not as frequent as now. One hardly saw them outside large and well-prepared expeditions with many porters. At the farms along the way, one called, "Milk?" "Eggs?" and if there was none of that, "Beans?" "Lentils?" but the people usually had only rice, which they polished and made useless, and lots of chili. If one had the bad luck that an expedition had just passed by, they often had no food at all. Gradually we became more hesitant about asking. After all, they could not eat the money we gave them, and with only a few square meters of terraced land to cultivate, they should not be given the possibility to sell too much of what they had. Of course, they all wanted money to spend on pocket lamps, which break and need expensive batteries, or ball-point pens, which are of no benefit to them at all.

What one should notice, when traveling in the Himalayas, is that outside towns, people prefer new bank notes and cannot return change on large ones. In 1970, that meant from ten rupees (one dollar) and up. It is useful to stock up on small and new bank notes before leaving Kathmandu. Also, the inhabitants of some valleys have no confidence in some of the coins, especially the half rupees. If at one stop they give a lot of a special kind of change, there is a good chance one will be unable to get rid of them the next time.

Everybody was helpful, patiently showing which unmarked paths were the right ones, and we could do something in return. At every village, people came streaming to the white visitors with their diseases. They were usually monstrous cases of goiter or influenza, infected wounds or headaches, and often a few drops of iodine and a Band-Aid solved everything. If one can teach them to give their children enough to drink when they have diarrhea, it is possible to save many lives without effort. A high percentage of children in Nepal never reach five years of age (at that time it was about sixty-five percent), and a doctor told us that most simply dry out. The parents think they should not have anything to drink when they have the runs.

Frequent moving obstacles on the path were gigantic walking bushes with little feet underneath: They were ladies carrying enormous bundles of leaves which the men had cut off the trees. These leaves, from the so-called grass trees, are stored for winter or famine and fed to the cows and goats. Though the trunks are left totally stripped down, a new harvest appears every year, and their gnarled forms give a Goya-like feeling to the landscape. Each valley had its own trip, its own atmosphere. Some were friendly, others aggressive, some proud and others of a very commercial bent. At the pass one could already feel what was coming up—which human games would now be dominant. Sometimes, most people in a valley had the same face; a strong man had tended to the ladies there sometime, and now they all belonged to the same family.

As already mentioned, on the second day, the path to the Sherpa country joined the old trail south from Tibet, and the many stupas, Buddha statues, and slate stone reliefs by the roadside were an artistic joy. As soon as the path branched off east, however, the area became boring again, and the days were mostly characterized by stops at Hindu homes one could not enter and a massive lack of experiences or excitement. Here one made miles and whetted one's appetite for what would come.

In Giri, a village down from a broad, beautiful, sloping valley, the Swiss cross local and European cows and send Nepal's best cheese to Kathmandu. There is even an airstrip where small planes can land. We stayed there in Swiss style, not cheap but civilized, and enjoyed their excellent bread after the last dry stretch.

On the following ascent, the feeling of the land changed markedly. We were now in an age-old Buddhist area, and things started happening which touched us. Somehow everything seemed meaningful, and we felt relieved, open, and glad.

Shortly after leaving town, still with a view of the valley behind us, a fully-grown bull came rushing down the narrow ledge. It wanted the whole path to itself. I pushed Hannah against the rock behind me and quickly pulled my Nepalese officer's knife from its scabbard, an amazing two-foot-long chopping instrument. Snorting, the animal raced directly past, apparently aiming but just missing us with its horns. It was out of control, and luckily I did not have to kill it. The incident sharpened our receptivity to the striking landscapes, with woods of symmetrical pine trees, so different from the eroded brown earth of the former days.

Towards noon, still on the ascent to a pass, a radiantly transparent four-armed apparition manifested in front of me. It was a moonstone-colored, human-like shape of energy and light, and it hovered above the path. I couldn't believe it, rubbed my eyes, and looked again, but the form stayed in the air for what seemed like hours while we trudged along. At that time, holograms were not known. Today I would describe it as that, only more clear, radiant, and indescribably beautiful. It was the main aspect of Loving Eyes (*Avalokiteshvara* in Sanskrit and *Chenrezig* in Tibetan), the united compassion of all Buddhas. It was the first time I consciously saw a Bodhisattva in this life and for so long, but instead of fully opening up to it, happy beyond words, I did not know what to think about such a presence. After describing it to Hannah several times, we decided it must be a sign that we were now entering a Buddhist area.

Just as darkness fell, the track led by a large wooden Sherpa house. Their prices for sleeping and food were double the usual, meaning the equivalent of fifty cents for two. As it was already getting dark, and we liked them, we decided to dig into our own provisions instead of arguing the price down, as is usual there. They and their house somehow felt very pure, and we could not get into the mood for squeezing them. When they later discovered we were students of Karmapa, they reduced their prices automatically, and we were glad to also share their food.

It became a cozy evening, and they wanted to know everything about our lamas in Kathmandu. Finally, they gave Hannah the meditation beads of an old and very realized yogini who had lived in the area. Winding them around her wrist, Hannah received the day's blessing. Amazed, she felt a heat flow up her arm to her heart and spread over her body. Later, when—more out of habit than conviction—I wanted to improve on an already good evening with a smoke, it felt completely wrong. For the first time a very unpleasant, wild heartbeat set in. This was Buddha country, and though I always forgot it quickly as it did not suit my philosophy, they evidently did not like hemp as incense.

The next day brought few passes to cross. The landscape was mainly open, and for hours there was a river on our right. The weather

The Chenrezig which turned pink and smiled on us
on the Buddha's Enlightenment Day at Swayambhu

was wet, rough, and stormy, often with large hail. It all fit, however. The Sherpas who beckoned us to take shelter in their homes were often interesting on a human level, and their altars were something else. Though very rustic in appearance, here the over-sized eyes and hands on their statues and *thankas* somehow fit. Peaceful, protective, female, male, single, and in union, these roughly hewn Buddha-forms are everywhere, blessing both the roads and the houses. Here there was no need to treat the people like children; one could have a real exchange. Even when there was not much to say or do, just being there was fine. Whenever they discovered our connection to Karmapa, they would not take any money for food or tea. Luckily we already knew the trick of leaving some rupees on the altar of their houses. It saved a lot of talking, and they could not refuse.

That day we did not get very far. There were too many visits. However, we must have stayed at the right place, because the next morning, they brought a child who was nothing but skin and bones. It was nearly dead. When I put the container with Karmapa's hairs on the top of its head, it opened its eyes and smiled. Whatever happened after that, the child's energies were now turned upwards, and it would go to a good state of existence.

Not until ten the next morning did we reach Bander, a tent-camp at the confluence of two mountain streams. It lies at only six hundred meters altitude. From here starts the ascent into the heartland of the Sherpas. People had described it in detail several times: One first walks three kilometers up to a pass, then follows a ridge for several hours, and finally descends some hundred yards through a forest. Another hour after that is a place where people live.

There was snow up there already, and although it was late, we would still have to finish before it got dark. People advised starting early the next morning, but Europeans have no time for waiting, and trusting the protection of our Buddhas, we just started out. The track zigzagged up an endless barren hillside and then passed through untouched landscape. The chirping of birds was constant, stopping abruptly when enormous eagles hovered overhead. Every bend of the road gave a new and wider view, and our tins of condensed milk supplied enough "quick-speed" for the body not to need rest on the way.

Halfway up stood a monastery, which we just could not pass by. It was guarded by a noisy Tibetan mastiff the size of a cow, but the Lama was educated and really nice. He enjoyed showing us the building and could answer every question about the exquisite Buddhas and scrolls. We could not stay long, however, if we wanted to find something with a roof that day.

Near the pass, with our shoes already soaked by the snow, a small horse caravan invited us to join them. They knew where to stay on the other side of the ridge and said that no one could make it the whole way to the Sherpa capital of Jumbesi before dark. It was another three hours' journey from the pass over ground that would likely break one's legs.

It was a historic chance. We had never been in a caravan before, and books by Chaucer and others soon came alive. Among free people, given outer conditions apparently produce similar human behavior, and it was all timeless and most interesting. What especially pleased us was the kindness they showed their animals. It was a very pleasant surprise after the tortures so many witness, especially in the Moslem countries. These Sherpas radiated good humor and inner peace and found it natural, which I then did not, when people we met on the pass came up and asked for my blessing. It was the first time this happened, and the reason was probably my hour-long vision of Loving Eyes, something truly extraordinary. I got around it by placing a picture-button of Karmapa and the container with his hairs on their crowns, and it was deeply satisfying to feel the power of the lineage flow through. The path along the ridge moved through an otherworldly rhododendron wood. It frequently offered views of valleys on both sides, and each one seemed more breathtaking than the last. As the sun disappeared behind the horizon, the caravan finally descended into the Sherpa valley. All were wet to the knees but happy.

More than thirteen tribes live in Nepal. They have hardly any intermingling, and each do their thing. Most of the Hindus subsist in straw huts, while others inhabit virtual museums, like the Buddhist Newaris. Their houses delight visitors in the town-centers of the Kathmandu valley. The Sherpas, a strong, active people, have built homes that would look good anywhere. Most of their roomy log cabins date back to the time when the goods from Tibet passed through their country. They then traded and also guided the caravans. When such jobs disappeared due to the Chinese destruction of Tibet, they found other outlets for their energy. They became leaders of the many Himalayan expeditions or traders in Kathmandu. Because of their willingness to move with opportunity, a relatively rare quality in tradition-bound Asian societies, and their extraordinary lungs, which enable them to work as high-altitude mountain guides, they frequently lose their young. This is all the more noticeable because, like the Tibetans and Bhutanese, they prefer their families small and educated. They are very unlike the other races in the area, who keep their women pregnant all the time, hoping to produce soldiers for Allah or enough money-earning male offspring for a secure old age. More than any other factor, this egotism clutters up and pollutes their formerly beautiful countries.

Just as it became too dark to continue, there was a light to the left, and our party was well received at what appeared to be the first farm on the way. Behind the main building was a fenced-in triangular field with a tall pole carrying a banner of victory. Sleeping in fresh hay, with the sound of horses and the flapping of prayer-flags, we had good and strong dreams.

The next morning the Sherpa family invited us to their meditation room. They had seen us meditate and now wanted to show us something. They opened the saddlebags, which they had made sure to carry in first on the previous evening, placing their contents on a table. Rarely had we seen such meticulously worked statues of Buddhas and high Lamas, but their faces had been smashed, apparently by the Chinese. They were serious pieces of art, and their intact base-plates meant that they still contained the blessings which add markedly to their usefulness as meditation aids. Mainly consisting of mantra rolls and relics from great yogis and charged up places, their energies can be felt by those who are open to them. "They will now get new faces," said the Sherpas, "and then we will take them to places where people understand what they are."

We were touched. Smuggling charged-up statues out of Tibet so they could be used for their true purpose was a great act. We also knew, however, that they might not stay in the temples for long. Unscrupulous traders paid gangs to steal statues all over the country, later selling them in the West. Here, they are frequently emptied by hash-seeking customs people or curious owners and stand around as exotic ornaments or investments in the houses of people who know nothing of their value for the mind. The minutes there were an excellent opportunity to understand the workings of Karma, to see how beings plant the seeds of either happiness or suffering for the future. Some results, however, do not only appear in future lifetimes. With help, Karma may ripen more quickly than that!

At that very time, all Kathmandu was talking about the trial of Chinni Lama's sons. Armed with guns, an unheard-of circumstance in Nepal, they had been caught during such a robbery. They were arrested the day after Karmapa had given Chinni Lama the white dress which we had understood as a support for his purification. As became evident during the trial, and as much of Nepal had known all along, the family had been prominent in quite a few fields.

The well-defined path to Jumbesi, the capital of the Sherpa country, was unpleasant to walk. For some reason, the farmers threw the rocks from their fields there. We dodged the worst leg-breakers, marching past idyllic log cabins and many, many stupas. There was no way one could ignore them. Recently we had heard that they contain ritual objects and relics, which charge up the whole environment. In Kathmandu one learns very quickly to walk with one's right shoulder towards them, moving around with the sun, clockwise.

Stupas are ever-present expressions of Buddhist cultures. All the different varieties are structured to explain the universe on outer, inner, and secret levels, and the texts insist that they have an ever-deepening influence on mind. They help transform beings' present "impure" experience of the world into the pure Buddha realm it really is. Sowing the seeds for seeing things as they really are, beyond expectation or fear, they bring forth a state where each event is true and perfect in itself. Thus, gradually, mind will recognize its original joy and freedom. Passing from conditioned to unconditioned states, it will move from confusion to enlightenment.

The square "angular" base of a stupa manifests the solid or "earth" aspect of the universe, and its color is a transparent yellow. It corresponds to the disturbing feeling of pride and the direction "South." In enlightenment, this feeling is transformed into the wisdom which shows the basic equality of all things, that everything outer and inner is, in its nature, conditioned and composite. The round, drop-shaped part above that symbolizes the water element, the "flowing" aspect of the universe. The color of this is a transparent blue, and it corresponds to the feeling of anger and the direction "East." As anger is transformed into mirror-like wisdom, it shows things as they are, neither adding nor withdrawing anything. The rectangular level above that represents "heat," the fire element, and the direction "West." Its color is transparent red. Representing egotistical desire, one's developing practice makes it into discriminating wisdom. This insight is the most relevant kind to happy people and recognizes things separately but at the same time as part of a totality. In Tibet and Nepal, this part is often (as with the stupas at Bodhnath and Swayambhu) decorated with eyes of wisdom, looking in the four directions. The tapering upper part with the rings symbolizes the element "air" or "movement" on the ordinary levels. It expresses itself through the color transparent green, the direction "North," and the feelings of envy and jealousy. Transformed by meditation, view, and life, these feelings become the wisdom of experience, also described as all-performing. The uppermost part of the stupa either depicts a sun inside of a crescent moon or is understood as representing the flaming drop of the space element inside a bowl holding the elixir of life. It is transparent radiant or moonstone-like, and in its impure state, it represents ignorance and dullness. Transformed indirectly during work with the former four disturbances, or very rarely through a direct approach, its all-pervading wisdom and intuitive insight dissolve any limits in time and space. These five wisdoms together constitute full enlightenment. They express themselves as fearless insight, spontaneous joy, and active compassion and bless all beings in peace-giving, enriching, fascinating, and protective ways. Known from Tibetan scrolls as the sitting, cross-armed, blue form of Dorje Chang, the holder of diamond-like enlightenment to the Kagyu Lineage, this mental state expresses itself through the lama and especially as the successive incarnations of Karmapa. Called the Great Seal, Chagchen, or Mahamudra, it is the original nature of every being, and remaining in this awareness at all times and places is full enlightenment.

The shoulder-high "mani"—walls dividing the paths in the Sherpa country—have the same purpose as the stupas. They carry inscriptions of Om Mani Peme Hung and other mantras in the five colors and display bas-reliefs of the most well-known Buddha-aspects. Thus even walking past them became a practice of opening one's mind.

Though one saw little real innovation, the area vibrated with Buddhist influence. Everything was part of a totality, and to the positive observer, different ways to meaningful levels of consciousness were presented very convincingly. Hannah and I enjoyed it thoroughly, felt surrounded and inspired by influences that we had come to trust and love. Excited and happy, we goaded sometimes the humans and then the caravan's horses to ever higher speeds.

After passing an especially large and newly colored mantra on a gigantic overhanging rock, the landscape suddenly opened up. Below was a wide valley with a cluster of about twenty houses, the capital of the Sherpa country, Jumbesi. Close by, on the left, was a single tall house on a lawn. A young Italian appeared from its doorway and ran up to us. He was living there in order to learn *thanka* painting and wanted to know whom we had met on the way. He seemed lonely and lost, knowing no Tibetan, and probably just wanted to know he was still alive. Some kilometers further behind the house and half hidden by a mountain, lay a majestic monastery which we felt strongly drawn towards. However, we had agreed to meet our Danish gang in town before making further plans, and so we went there first. They were in neither of the two eating places but had already made themselves exceedingly well known. They had managed to empty Jumbesi of Chang, the homemade beer, and were now on a tour for a few days to dry up the surrounding area. We also learned that it was Tuchi Rinpoche's monastery we had wanted to go to. So, having now kept our promise, we left a message, with most of our luggage, for our friends and started up the hill quickly. We wanted to see the Lama whom Chechoo Rinpoche had so strongly recommended.

It was an idyllic walk up between the mountains, with changing weather and a landscape like an English park. The monastery was built in typical Tibetan fashion, and somebody must have been generous; like several of the mantras on the way, it shone with a coating of fresh paint. The back of the main building leaned against the mountain, and in front was a central courtyard, surrounded by a wall. Small, one-story row houses were built around and beneath it, quarters for lamas, monks, and nuns. On the rock-side above, quite a ways up and to the right of the main buildings, some intriguing small meditation huts were built into the mountain. Here yogis spend months and sometimes years in retreat. Often these huts are so small that one can only sit there, but although they may seem a place of terrible torment to an outside observer, they are places of great bliss to meditators. To them such a situation offers the opportunity to avoid outer confusion, to turn mind inward, and realize its nature. Nothing but mind can experience fulfillment, and with the right teaching, that spontaneous joy may arise which is everybody's timeless essence.

Also this monastery was guarded by an enormous and noisy dog, but it was smart enough to retreat after a few well-aimed stones. Nothing could silence the shrieking ravens everywhere, so we had to knock on the door for quite a while before somebody peeked out at us.

After hearing that we were Karmapa's students and had been sent by Lama Chechoo, the monk fully opened the door. He was visibly glad and took us straight to the kitchen where tea was ready. In Tibetan houses and monasteries this is where most activities are planned, and, if one is not disturbed by the smoke from the fireplace, often so acrid that no Western eyes can bear it, Tibetan-style kitchens are nice. The monk was a natural genius. He could imitate anybody, also the unpleasant visa officers in Kathmandu, the horror of all visitors. We rolled with laughter. It was completely unexpected to meet someone with such humor and mimicry in an area where people looked as if hewn from gray granite. He also shared their story. Together with Tushi Rinpoche and some monks, he had fled the advancing Chinese from just north of Mt. Everest. He showed us a wall painting of the former monastery, now destroyed, as well as something completely new: Karmapa in the posture of giving maximum blessing. The soles of his feet and palms of his hands were stretched completely towards one.

We were glad to have kept some aspirins, Band-Aids, and iodine as gifts for such events. Then he took us to a richly decorated room where we could stay. He said, "Rinpoche has just withdrawn for six months to meditate. He is sitting upstairs where no one can visit him. However, you are welcome here and should make yourselves at home in every way."

Shortly before going on this trek, we had received our first Diamond Way meditation in English. The sender was a Chinese yogi in Kalimpong, a town in the eastern Himalayas. This yogi had first surprised us a bit with the kind of books he wanted from Denmark. In the fashion of those innocent days, they depicted that female beauty which made the joys of our country known in many parts of the world. We were still wondering what use naked ladies could be to him. Could there be some subtle difference in the inner channels in Western and Eastern bodies? Well, whatever it was, he had sent us a fine gift. A translated meditation on Green Liberatrice, Dolma (Tara), the female compassion of all Buddhas, lay well protected in my rucksack. At that time everything was in Tibetan, so it was a real treasure.

Although we did not know it, our Buddhist status lacked the official stamp. During Karmapa's visit, for two months we had floated from one Crown Ceremony and initiation to the next. His power had kept us dazed, but nobody had brought the initial step of taking Refuge to our attention. Even without formally being Buddhists, of course, we were, and it felt completely right to mentally create the perfect form of Green Liberatrice and use her vibration, "Om Tare Tuttare Ture Soha." More difficult was the identification of our moving minds with her unchanging Buddha-essence. She was really good to us, however, and we felt extraordinary waves of blessing and love.

Since enlightenment had still not struck the next morning, I thought we should improve on a good experience by using the very pure acid we had brought along. Hannah took double, and I took several times the ordinary dose; then we set out. Our goal was a small landing on the bare mountainside, a few hundred meters above the monastery. It looked ideal for meditation. The LSD started working very quickly, already on our way up. The steep, sandy path with the rocks sliding down came alive. The landscape started breathing, and then we were there. Meditating above the monastery, in the clear sun and with a great view over the Sherpa country, there was only joy. Again and again we dissolved the distant mountains into ourselves and breathed them out again. The powerful elemental energies of red copper and yellow brass came up to us through the gray rock. One level of meaning changed into the next, while atoms and cells vibrated with immense bliss. Suddenly I noticed that the horseflies had found us, or maybe they had been there the whole time. I let the first fly get his fill. It was a great joke that it might now get on an unexpected trip, and actually it did make some funny loops when flying away. When, however, the next fly sat down for a meal, without thinking, I flattened it. There I was then, with a flat, still slightly moving horsefly on my arm, and now the good feeling had gone. In spite of the power to let worlds appear and disappear, there was no compassion for a small animal. Seeing that was very disturbing.

When we climbed back down to the monastery in the evening, the acid was still active. After the horsefly, however, I was no longer at ease. There was some understanding tied up inside which wanted to express itself. Descending past a couple of Sherpas building a cabin, to my eyes they looked ugly and dwarfish. I knew that one's outer experience is a reflection of one's inner state; therefore, this was not a good sign. So the question was how to best phase out the trip, how to re-enter normal consciousness as a friendly man with the greatest amount of positive impressions as ongoing motivation. In this searching state, shortly before reaching the monastery, we noticed a small tree with bundles of meditation texts tied to it. They were old, worn out ones, not readable during the ceremonies anymore. Apparently they had been hung there to spread their good energies to all beings. Of course, the practical compassion behind that action was the key. Nothing else had real importance. Realizing that, all inner tightness dissolved. With tears of thankfulness in my eyes, over and over I repeated the promise to work for these precious teachings. With Hannah at my side, we deeply vowed to spread the methods that balance the unconditioned power just tasted with the greatest of wisdom and love.

Entering the monastery, we strengthened this deep wish in front of the Buddhas, and it stayed. We both see it as having roots in the past and continuing into future lives, and actually, it is nothing but common sense: if we think of ourselves, we have problems. Thinking of others, there are countless exciting situations to tackle.

Our countrymen were back in Jumbesi. They had finished whatever beer they could find in the surroundings and now expected the town people to have brewed some more. It was good to see them again, and all had lots to tell. With amazing speed, they had become a part of this Sherpa village. Their Viking habits had been accepted, and there was no distance from the locals. Recently they had talked to a historian about the history of the Sherpas, and the summary was like this:

Starting in the fourteenth century, the Sherpas came down in three waves, with a few hundred years between, covering the area where they now live. They came from Eastern Tibet, now the province of Kham, and had apparently been driven out by warlike tribes of newcomers, partially of European origin. These latest Khampas are the tough Tibetans. Even today they resist the ruthless Chinese army, and half are said to be robbers and half to be saints. Here, in the protective Himalayan valleys, the Sherpas retained some very earthy practices which were hardly known in Tibet any more. Very popular were weeklong celebrations with drinking, music, and religious dancing day and night.

These feasts are more than binges. They remove aggressions and feelings of separation. Presiding lamas direct the awakened energies, and due to their skill, the Sherpas share experiences of their fundamental oneness. Thus these active people have become peaceful, and their society is held together. The lamas are from the "old" school of Tibetan Buddhism as well as from Karmapa's lineage, and many have women. Being powerful teachers, they can enjoy worldly happiness and transcend it at the same time.

In Jumbesi all knew that Tuchi Rinpoche had withdrawn for another half-year of retreat, that he was now meditating to transform the negativity of a dangerous world. The people there live in the context of the Refuge. It is the certainty that there is an absolute goal, full enlightenment, Buddhahood; that ways lead there, Buddha's teachings or Dharma; and that they can trust their friends on the way (Sangha). Whoever wants to use effective methods for quickest results also needs the refuge in the lama, the teacher. He (she) is the source of confidence, spiritual power, and activity.

It is this certainty of an absolute refuge that inspires not only well-established Sherpas, but also the poorest Tibetan refugees. These days an increasing number of practicing Westerners manifest that same unshakable quality which proves one's basic mental health. It is an intuitive warmth which appears when mind is no longer attached to expectation or fear. When its spontaneous energy can work beyond either-or confrontations and is able to see the world from the viewpoint of both/and, this quality naturally arises.

Everywhere, the houses were built of gray, rough-hewn stones and full-timber planks. They were stately and easy to enter. Each one had a prominent room for the Buddhas, and several were used only for practice, otherwise standing empty. The latter kind often had yards for ceremonial dances. Surrounded by roughly made wooden fences, they were very different from the delicately carved work of the Kathmandu valley. Many of the statues on the altars were hundreds of years old, and like many of the scrolls along the way, they had the unmistakable sign of having been produced in the countryside and not in town: Hands and eyes were oversized and stomachs were extremely long.

One entered and left Jumbesi between stupas, and everywhere the power of Guru Rinpoche pervaded. He is the fully accomplished yogi who brought Buddhism to Tibet. This "precious teacher," also called Padma Sambhava or Pema Jungne, "Lotus-Born," held the highest initiations of tantric Buddhism. From an area which is today inside Afghanistan, around year 741, he brought the vision of absolute, beyond-ego enlightenment to Tibet, together with many Diamond Way methods for obtaining it. He left his legacy with one of his main wives, but as the shamans destroyed Buddhism across the country shortly after, little but his manifold "hidden treasures" are left today. They can only be taken out by non-celibate lamas and are always discovered when they are useful to the spirit of the time. His teachings are considered genuine by the three "old" or Red Hat schools of Buddhism but not by the Yellow-Hat or "Virtuous" Gelugpa school, which governed Tibet.

After a few days, with seven or eight of the gang, we started off on a tour of the Sherpa country. Moving at an average altitude of 3000 meters, we planned a big circle of their heartland, visiting the important sites and monasteries. The only ones to avoid were the famous Tangboche and Pangboche, base-camps for attempts on Mount Everest. Two major expeditions, Australian and Japanese, had eaten everything on the way—pushing the prices of food to ridiculous levels.

We left by the lower road, taking one past the largest stupa in town, crossed a stream to the left on slippery planks, and started up a hillside. The path wound through untouched woods and a breathtaking landscape. Every bend brought new views, and whether look-ing far or near, there was enough to catch one's eyes.

At most houses, the people invited us inside and offered food. They asked for news, and our things were fingered and discussed. We could have traded our foam-mats five times over and everything else at least once at nearly every stop. The relics Karmapa had given us they at once put on top of their heads, thus transferring his energy to themselves. Most asked where he was now staying and proudly said that this or that uncle or aunt had seen the Black Crown in Kathmandu and received his blessing.

The culinary joys were severely limited. Sherpas mainly eat potatoes, which they throw into the embers of the fireplace, pull out by hand, and eat. They also have roasted barley-flour, called tsampa, which they mix with tea and make into a kind of paste called tsampa. In many cases today, they have to make do with wheat, maize, or even soybeans. This traditional staple is one of the best-known things about their culture, and it is said that where there is confidence in the lamas and tsampa is eaten, that is Tibet. Sometimes there is also yogurt, and if Moslems live nearby to butcher the animals or when they fall and die by themselves, the Sherpas have meat. One can scare them away with vegetables! Many Tibetans were not introduced to such substances until in exile. Also today, many think that green things are only for cows.

There are several ways to make tsampa. Usually one throws grains into a cauldron of hot sand and moves the mixture around until it pops. Then the sand is sifted off, and the grains are put in a bag and danced upon until the shells come off. Finally, everything is thrown into the wind, and what remains is ground into fine flour. The "tea," which is drunk in gigantic quantities, has a bad reputation, mainly because Westerners have completely different associations to the word. To Tibetans it is a soup of milk, salt, and butter, with as much low-grade tea added as is necessary to kick some taste through. Especially on the chests of these highlanders, it deposits a layer of protective fat against the biting winds and cold. Understood as five o'clock tea, it is a horror, but as a soup, it is not so bad. Also the frequent claim of travel-books that the butter must be rancid is not true. The Sherpas definitely prefer fresh butter, but people who live on the very edge of subsistence must eat what they can get. Having an experience with the evil substance a few days later, however, we understood well that whoever tries it does not easily forget.

One very elementary device would have humanized every indoors—the chimney. No matter which house we entered, after only a few minutes, tears ran and all fled the open fireplace. The smoke is supposed to leave through a hole in the roof, which appears by pushing a shingle to the side. Its location depends on the strength and direction of the wind, but the system clearly does not function. Also, there seems to be excessive acid in the wood they burn; even without visible smoke, the tears keep running.

While we Westerners rubbed our eyes, the Sherpas didn't seem to mind. Altogether, they were not squeamish. They pulled glowing pieces of charcoal from the fire with their bare hands and carried copper cauldrons, without handles, full of boiling water. Their lifestyle, physical build, and facial structure all struck us as being neither very individualized nor sensual, although the variety of their daily experience was probably larger than that of modern man in sheltered "consuming" situations. Somehow the Sherpas seemed to have grown right out of the gray rocks, and the few "modern" types clearly stood out, such as the monk who could imitate the visa people.

Here, like everywhere in Nepal, people wanted to buy the Gurkha-knife on my belt, while I politely tried to switch the conversation to something else. Though most knives sold in Nepal are of good quality, being made from the springs of lorries, this was an officer's chopping instrument of amazing balance, which could even cut down a small tree. Countless hammerings and temperings of these genuine ones direct the steel molecules of the blade in a forward direction, and a test of this is that the edge of one knife will take a bit off the back of another without being nicked. Traditionally, these knives should be given a taste of blood each time they leave the scabbard, and Gurkha soldiers keep a small wound on a finger open always for that reason. This one is now with my brother in his self-built house in the woods of southern Sweden.

The first part of the way was slow. John, a disciple of the Hindu swami, insisted on his unhandy robes. He also wanted to be more native than the natives, walking barefooted on ground where they were happy to wear shoes. So after running circles around him for a while and studying the vegetation right and left, we went ahead. It was great to be in tennis shoes and have reduced packs.

The landscape was alive with reminiscences of Milarepa, the most famous of Tibetan yogis. He had meditated in this area nine hundred years ago, and his blessing had followed me since the inner-heat practice in the forgotten valley. The locals pointed out several caves where he had meditated. Since that time the power of his full enlightenment and the spontaneous beauty of his songs have benefited countless beings. The books about him, like *Tibet's Great Yogi Milarepa*, *Drinking from the Mountain Stream*, and *The Hundred Thousand Songs of Milarepa*, are impressive landmarks in Tibetan Buddhism, and his development as a human being never ceases to inspire. Such life stories tell more about the goal and way of Diamond Way Buddhism than dozens of learned treatises.

The area felt unchanged from his time, as was the life of the people, except for a bit of plastic and a few technical improvements. Two ways led up to Tjuang, an old, very large monastic complex high above the valley. We took the short, steep one for climbers and were suddenly surrounded by temples.

Around the main monastery-buildings were the usual small meditation huts. There were also plateaus where specially trained yogis meditated to dissolve the much-feared hailstorms at harvest time. They did this with amazing success, while blowing their long horns and conches. Hailstorms are no joke up there. The stones can reach the size of eggs, kill people and livestock, and easily destroy crops. The monastery itself was run-down and desolate. Few monks and nuns were staying there now, and the exceedingly fine art in the halls was in total disrepair. Unlike Ladakh and west-central Tibet, where the dry, high-altitude air preserves buildings and art for centuries as long as no foreign invaders or cultural revolutions interfere, the climate here is quite moist. Once a roof leaks, fungus appears quickly, and unprotected things just rot away. All in all, the area around the monastery had a depressed feeling. As there were no powerful lamas there anymore to hold the people, even the farmers had moved to more inspiring places.

Richard, an American, had studied for a while at Tjuang. He was one of the first Westerners to regularly use Diamond Way meditations and felt much benefit. His attempts at a meditative life, how-

Dorje and bell.
Ritual implements
signifying the union
of male-female,
of compassion-wisdom,
of space and bliss

ever, were thwarted by thirsty Danes much too often, and he was easily swayed by them! As we arrived, he was visited upon by Jan "the General," a very insistent guest. Jan's total clarity of vision as to which house in the valley was now brewing beer was only surpassed by his endless diligence in carrying two big buckets, full to the brim with fermented barley-soup, up the long, winding road. Some joked that if he had used those same qualities for meditation, the world would have a great teacher today.

There was only time for one night in Tjuang, and in the morning, Hannah bought the small Dorje and meditation-bell of a deceased nun. We paid $7, too much for that time. It had not yet dawned upon us that many of the robed ones, like most people in Asia, are born traders. Thus we did not bargain, as was expected, but paid what was asked and even felt a blessing in doing so. Even now, when we know them better, it feels strange to trade with monks. A lot of unique things came together, however, and these meditation-supports and blessed objects now give atmosphere to our Diamond Way meditation centers around much of the world.

With a far view of the valley, the path led on to the Taxindu monastery. The winds and fog from Mount Everest enveloped everything, and the ice-wall of a gigantic mountain appeared on the left whenever it was possible to see for any distance. On the long rise, a low wooden hut lay by the road. Here lived an astonishing elderly yogini in ragged red robes who was reputed to always have milk and yogurt. I couldn't take my eyes off her. She had that refined, slightly nervous female energy, which attracted me so strongly ever since childhood and always so activates my protective feelings.

Here again, right by Mount Everest, was a totally modern type who might have been leading a ladies' circle in Copenhagen or creating important art in one field or another. I had a rare bout of homesickness looking at her, and thought of my mother, the workings of Karma, and what actions get us born here or there. Taxindu lies in the last pass before Namche Bazaar and base camp. The icy peaks, which sometimes appear between the constantly rising clouds, seem to be at touching distance, while the landscape changes from one moment to the next. Since being there, a wish has remained to one day do a longer retreat at this place.

The head lama was a joyful, young incarnate, who either no longer distinguished between the conditioned and unconditioned worlds, or was not very interested in teaching us Buddhism. Anyway, he avoided our questions, and right after an invocation with an impressive use of ceremonial instruments, he started offering us cultural objects to buy. For once we became judgmental, nearly moralistic. We did not realize that he probably needed money for his monastery and that he had no doubt tried to explain Buddha's teachings to disinterested Westerners before. Instead of being grateful for the treasures offered and his reasonable prices, we at once classified him as a "money-lama" and were not receptive to the mildness and openness which he radiated. We wound up with a well-painted, power-field "mandala" of Diamond Mind, the purifying energy of all Buddhas, and some very beautiful copper objects for altars.

The last place on the tour of the Sherpa country was the Tibetan refugee camp of Jalsa. On the way lay the small temple of the lama who came to Kathmandu to make rain, the one from whom Buddha Laximi had obtained our first protectors. He wasn't there but his family was, and we left them an offering as thanks for all the trouble he had kept us out of. Until today his good wishes have followed our series of used but fast German cars and motorcycles, making them nearly invisible to speed traps and giving them amazing life-spans. In spite of outer poverty, the feeling in the camp was excellent, a thing one can generally expect from Tibetans until they get involved in politics. The houses had altars with statues of Buddha-aspects and lamas, and charged up "prayer" flags fluttered in all colors between trees and poles. Through open doorways one saw colorful Tibetan carpets being woven by chatting ladies. They were glad; the people from population control had just distributed condoms, and they could now make love without getting pregnant. At nearly every turn of the track here we bumped into old acquaintances from Karmapa's visit in Kathmandu.

Sitting with them in the canteen of the refugee-camp, I had an experience which some consider a flashback from an earlier life, while others see it as mind's double reaction to some sensory input. Until such events can be objectively verified, it is wise not to have too many fixed ideas about them. Anyway, looking through the door into the setting sun, the characteristic silhouettes of three tall Khampa-warriors stood out against the flaming red evening sky. I recognized having seen exactly that before. It could only have been in Tibet.

From Jalsa we took the short cut to Jumbesi to pick up the rest of our luggage. The monsoon was now on its way, and it was necessary to return to Kathmandu at once. In a forced march of four days, with Hannah's long legs dancing nimbly and mine plodding along under the luggage, we reached Lamsango just as the bus was leaving. The very same evening we were in that metropolis of impressions known as Kathmandu. Possibilities, which had been latent in the space of the mountains, were now taking form everywhere.

CHAPTER EIGHT

The Last Trip

SOME BAD NEWS WAS WAITING IN KATHMANDU. We had already applied for a visa to Sikkim a month before Karmapa's departure, and now, two months later, the interior ministry in Delhi had sent a flat "no." It was clear obstruction. The thought of being separated from Karmapa by some incompetent Indian bureaucrats was really too much. In addition, there were some very practical considerations. Although Buddha Laxími, helpful as always, had found us a fine room next to Lama Chechoo's house, the best possible for our situation, we were not only running out of money fast, but also our Nepalese visas would soon be out. However, we did not want to go back to Europe. It was certain that we had not yet learned enough.

In jail, I had let my hair grow long for the first time. During the years of smuggling, there had been good reasons to keep it short and look anonymous. It was actually pleasant when it tickled my shoulders, and it did make me milder. So for a while I kept my hair long. The only disadvantage was that it matted easily. One day, while washing it, I decided that it took too much time. I would now have it all shaved off. Surfacing from the barber-shop near the fire-tower with a respectable white egg for a head, nicely scarred from my earlier life, Terry came bicycling past. Cool as always, he said, "Listen, you're university trained, aren't you? Would you like to teach English for the American Embassy?" Straightness pays. Here was our chance to stay. Such a job would supply both a visa and some needed money, so of course I said "yes."

Thus, Hannah and I became Nepalese residents for half a year. We belonged to the small group of privileged people who could live and even earn money in this paradise. The ever tighter visa laws and the obligatory sums of money to be exchanged at the official bank-rate each month no longer affected us. The "school" was the language lab on top of the American library on New Road, and I went there for a few hours a day on the few days each week that were not religious or national holidays. It was also fun. My students, who needed their English to study agriculture at universities, mainly in the third world, were curious, intelligent, and expert cheaters.

Our fixed income was 800 rupees—then about forty dollars a month. This was enough to live on, help others, buy Tibetan religious things, and even have some left. Our only worry was that Hannah had some strange stomach disease. The Russian hospital could not figure out what it was, but I wonder if they could detect a pregnancy in the ninth month! Otherwise, we were in good shape and unaffected even by the monsoon, which weakened nearly everybody. After a while I was also hired by the Russian Embassy to teach English and German to one of their bigwigs, and it was quite a funny situation. The Russians paid better, and I was always picked up right in front of the American Embassy by one of their ZIL limousines. They were big, strong people but visibly unhappy; half the work was making them trust the high level of education they already had and simply talk.

Weekends were often spent at the Tibetan border, meditating for the destroyed country and bathing in the hot springs there. Though our focus and way of thinking had not changed, much to our surprise, we gradually became a meeting-ground for the different worlds and generations in and around Kathmandu. It was strange to be depended upon by the bourgeois people we had always tried to avoid and even stranger to frequently discover qualities in them which our generation badly needed.

Rubi was an excellent mate of ours. He was the black Tibetan mini-dog of our very intelligent host-family. One evening he ate condensed milk containing some tiny flakes of hash and totally lost it:. He sat tilted at an angle and gazed at us for hours, sensing that only we knew what was happening to him. Staying up all night, we took him through the experience, and neither confusion nor fear appeared in his mind. Though Rubi could not talk, the process was strangely similar to our usual work as trip-guides with humans. From then on, he had unending confidence in us and apparently decided to simply come along, giving me the job of protecting him from hordes of jealous street dogs. It became a time for learning a lot about dogs and about gray-zones in one's mind: had I just kicked them out of compassion or irritation?

Daily we invoked Karmapa's power-field from the picture on our wall, used our bells to focus our mind, and made deep wishes until we felt it coming alive. We would not accept that the bums in Delhi had refused our Sikkim-visa and collected information on going in and out without papers. Then Chechoo Lama advised us to try the legal way again. We did so, applying this time for only a few days as tourists, but the certainty of another month-long wait felt wrong. Though outwardly in great shape, inwardly we weren't satisfied. In the evenings we frequently received Lama Chechoo's blessing, mostly on smoke-filled, red-eyed heads. But he didn't give us more than that.

One evening, he called us. "This is it," we thought excitedly. "Finally he will give an initiation like in the books on Milarepa." But the Lama only wanted us to sell some wooden cups for a Bhutanese monk who needed money. Walking the few steps back to our house, we felt empty and cheated.

A delayed letter arrived, saying that on my birthday in March, a German hippie had burned our flat in historical Copenhagen. It had been the excellent base for many inner and outer trips. But Lopon Chechoo just smiled and said, "Good, fire purifies." And shortly thereafter also our Nepalese altar burned while we were at a feast. Everything on it was ashes except for a picture of Karmapa and some LSD. It had been given to us as a gift because nobody knew how strong it was.

In this spiritual vacuum, one evening we took the acid. Now, at least, something would happen. We interpreted the acid not burning as a sign to take it and especially expected the pressure behind our foreheads to now become clarity. The acid was very strong, even for us, and came on very quickly. We left our bodies and moved around in the vicinity, returned, moved around again, and meditated on Padma Sambhava. Towards morning, when making love, a power field of rhombic shapes in metallic colors appeared, and I had the feeling that it wanted to make Hannah pregnant. I kept it away, but the trip went on. Some hours later in the language laboratory, the rhombic metallic forms were still there. My voice was too rough to speak clearly, so while lecturing on the economic importance of the oil recently found along the coast of Norway, I had the idea of drinking some ginseng solution from the Chinese export shops in Kathmandu.

Though a lack of time and imagination have saved me from most diseases, I knew that ginseng is very healthy. So I drank the entire bottle at once, though the dosage was only a few drops. At that moment, a strange energy moved into my throat, and the rhombic pattern was gone. It felt as if I had been put back several years, into my time of boxing and weekly fights. Again, I caught myself being provocative. And so I made a drama, which would not have been relevant a few days earlier.

On the way from the Tibetan border, this time we sat behind the front window of a completely new Tata bus, with a simplified Mercedes motor built on license in India. After so long in the slow East, I was ecstatic about feeling such a beautiful piece of machinery humming underneath us. What I was not enjoying, however, was the fact that the driver, a tall and powerful looking former Gurkha soldier, was doing everything in his might to ruin it. Like other drivers there, he earned extra money by picking up whatever stood by the roadside, so soon the coach was completely filled with people and animals, and some were even piled on the roof. Several times I informed him that if he overloaded the car, he would have to run the brand new motor at alternating revolutions or it would be destroyed. He understood me perfectly but didn't care.

So it happened as expected. A piston seized, and the driver just managed to free-wheel the bus down a slope to the beginning of a village. He climbed out to look at the damage, and I got in front of him and said, "It is your fault that we're stuck. We need another bus, so give us the rest of our money back." The driver was angry, and as he grasped my shirt with his oily hands, I threw him into the ditch. He came up and tried again, and once more I helped him into the ditch. As he came the third time, he held an iron bar, but the people from the bus restrained him. I dropped the rucksack that I would have caught his punch with, and it was good that things stopped there. Since he was coming at me with a weapon, I would have damaged him quite a bit.

It was a sobering situation! People did not know about our conversation, and with a shaved head, beads around my neck, and a button with Karmapa's picture on my T-shirt, I had just roughed up what was to their eyes an unfortunate bus driver in a most uncompassionate way. With all glances zeroing in on me, I let the beads and the picture of Karmapa, to whom I had done so little honor, quickly disappear into a pocket. Making myself as invisible as possible, I slid backwards into a local teahouse, but somehow the bad vibrations followed. Everybody shied away from the otherwise jovial white man, and even the dogs seemed afraid to eat what I gave them. Having returned to Kathmandu in the evening, we went straight to the Lama and told him what had happened. As I explained the rhombic pattern with the metallic colors, he said, "Oh yes. That one I know. He always makes trouble. I will take care of him." Until late at night, we heard his bell and drum, his chant invoking protective energies, and the next morning I woke up with tears of joy in my eyes. The "thing" had gone. I felt liberated from a heavy burden.

A few days before new moon in September 1970, good karma and blessings met. Suddenly, all things seemed to pull and push us towards Sikkim. One of the heavy visa police remembered us. In Nepal during those years, one rarely met totally unpleasant people outside this office. At our first meeting some years earlier, I had shaken him up a bit because he had not been respectful towards Hannah, and now he had been promoted. The upper officials there regularly lose their jobs when it becomes too evident that their wealth is increasing in no relation to their minimal pay. It means that they are selling the visas. Anyway, this gentleman was now in a position to revenge himself, and we were given a week to leave the country. What should we do? Lean on the Americans or Russians? Activate the Lama? We knew that he had more power in Nepal than even the embassies, that the royal family, though Hindu, was counting on his power to transfer their minds at the moment of death. Or should we just fix our own visas, using the classic method with the boiled egg? While still weighing the different possibilities, news came from Delhi that our papers for Sikkim had been issued at long last.

Under loads of gifts from Tibetan friends for Karmapa and his Lamas, a few days later we set out for Sikkim. By Tibetan custom, the traveler is also the mailman. The benefit is that one is always welcome, if not stopped by thieves or a broken back. Some Danes promised to bring the scrolls, statues, and other meditation-objects we had collected during our stay back to Europe in their VW bus. They appeared just in time, as there was no way we could bring these things along. Our departure was a night-long celebration with our inner core of friends, and we smoked so much that I walked sideways for most of the next day. In this state, none of us noticed that the bag with our books was stolen on the train. Climbing out of the window on some North Indian station to avoid stepping on the people lying at the door, I smashed one of the thermos bottles we had been asked to bring along. The thermos was a pity, but we took the disappearance of the books as a sign that a mere intellectual involvement with the Diamond Way was now over.

Hannah was already certain that our vast consumption of hash was probably not so useful for our development, that maybe it had kept us from getting any initiations from Lama Chechoo. Later, we found out that Karmapa had told him to mainly "hold" us, claiming us as his—meaning Karmapa's—personal students. But Hannah was surely right, too. Although he would have left the important steps to Karmapa, probably he would have taught us something had we only understood earlier that smoking and spiritual development clash— that one spreads the mind and the other concentrates it. On our way to Karmapa, however, we had the good sense to give away everything from our smoking time in Nepal, taking neither treasured implements nor even the smallest piece along.

Thus, the nine years of my life (for Hannah it was about half that much) offered on the altar of drugs were finally over. It was a gigantic, unexpected feeling of awakening and freedom to be able to just stop. Though some long-term effects may stay with me, always making something rattle (joke) when I shake my head, at least the initial step had been taken. Also to our own amazement, we have never wanted to touch the stuff again.

CHAPTER NINE

We Take Refuge in Buddha

LIKE ALL JOURNEYS on the North Indian Railways, the trip to Sikkim takes one to another world. After a few weeks of traveling the system, an author with a broad narrative style would have the material for a fascinating book. Actually, it is less a system of transportation than the existential background for countless Indians who live in, from, on, underneath, between, and around the trains. No aspect of basic human existence is hidden there.

To follow the Himalayas east, one first goes south by shaky local trains and later enters the infamous "Assam Mail." The villages along the way usually consist of a few huts of straw and bamboo. In the malaria-infested jungle just below the foothills, one understands how three English expeditions on their way to conquer Nepal had simply disappeared, and going east from there, one wishes that the white man had not given the locals penicillin without contraceptives. The enormously overpopulated lowlands, which spread from the Khyber pass at the Afghani border and way into Burma, would have been a paradise at about one tenth of the human density. Only some small mountains at Bodh Gaya and Rajgir, where the Buddha taught, jut out like nipples from a wide chest and break the monotony.

As the scenery changed, so did our co-travelers. First the small, dark forms of the malaria-resistant pre-Arian Indians were everywhere. At that time, few even thought of tickets on these stretches, as the conductors did not dare enter the trains. Gradually, however, as one enters the area where the vast north Indian towns lie, this type of humanity fades out. Now, the taller, light-skinned, "European"

Indians occupied every available inch of space. Around 3,000 years ago, these people came down from what is today Ukraine and pushed the original dark-skinned population into the corners of the country, occasionally mixing with them and producing races like the Biharis.

These "Ukrainians" protected their gene pool through the Vedas and Upanishads and built the fundamentally exclusive Hindu culture, which the world today experiences as typically "Indian." A caste system enforcing a tight net of social levels and rules of behavior was found useful to maintain control under the given conditions, and inside that, Buddha belonged to the warrior cast. Though most today imagine him with very "Asian" features, the texts describe him as tall, strong, and with blue eyes.

Moving at a snail's pace through these thousands of kilometers quickly becomes boring, and one is glad to have things to read and mantras to say. For two days the film moving past our windows was a variation of flatland, straw huts, and palms, enormous trees with hanging air roots, and temples in decay. White emaciated cows with wide horns—but well treated, as the Hindus consider them gods—pull simple, sometimes wooden, plows and big-wheeled carts that do not get stuck in the mud. People, people, people, most in white and many begging, complete the picture.

We had the feeling that half of India was in and around the train, and if we did not keep strictly to ourselves, but looked around normally, at least a hundred times a day somebody would ask, "Which country do you belong from?" The people had a real need to communicate, which we would have supported, but their English usually did not go beyond this question which they probably learned from friends. We could answer anything—lower Slobovia, the moon, or whatever—and they would all nod their heads sagely while the old ones would say, "Oh, England," and the young ones would say, "Oh, America." A wild-haired Indian, possibly a great existentialist guru in perfect disguise, came jumping into the compartment. He stared at us, shouted, "Where are you?" and was gone again.

Getting off the train at Siliguri, two days east of Kathmandu, once again we were surrounded by the smiling round faces and energetic small bodies of the mountain people. People spoke a Nepalese that we understood, and the vibrations became calm. There was no more yelling and screaming, and the joy of soon being with Karmapa could again grow.

On the second floor of the station, after stepping over people sleeping on papers and thin sheets everywhere, we got the so-called "inner-line" permit, a paper required for going to Darjeeling in the eastern Himalayan foothills. It was never checked on the way up but had to be shown to prolong one's stay or travel into really restricted areas like Sikkim. The policeman was asleep and had to be roused, so everything took a while. Fortunately, they were holding the last jeep for us. It provided what turned out to be a luxury ride.

Only six or seven people were going, whereas in Nepal traveling with 23 grownups, a few children, and several sacks of rice packed in one VW bus was considered quite normal. Another pleasant surprise was the newness of the jeep. We had come to think that they were produced "old." In a short while it too would look like the seemingly ancient Land Rovers, which stop every ten kilometers for different repairs. But for now, it was a joy that the driver did not have to turn the steering wheel twice before anything happened out front.

The road up alternates between one and two lanes and is often crossed by the tracks of an old mini-railroad that was built in Scotland late last century. Apparently the engineers for the road and those who made the tracks had shared a difficult relationship. The jeep had to wait several times for the toy-size train to pass, and the unmarked crossings were rough. Every jolt was getting us nearer to Karmapa, however, so we were not complaining.

From Siliguri, for a long time the road runs straight through lowlands dotted with tea estates, then it winds upwards through a subtropical rain forest. The region borders on Assam, the wettest place in the world, where between 13 and 17 meters of rain fall every year, all in just a few months. After about two hours of hairpin curves with a few wooden horses along the road, our driver stopped across from the train station at Kurseong. It lies about 1,000 meters above sea level and is the first town after Siliguri. With teacakes and a fine view over the plains, it is a pleasant stop. From there the road climbs the same distance on to Sonada, where so much of importance would later happen. Another winding eight kilometers with a fine view to the left, take one up to a pass. Ghoom, the town here, is about two and a half kilometers up. As it is mostly covered by clouds, many locals imitate the English and call it "Gloom."

Shortly before the pass, the only road on the whole stretch branches off. The driver said that it soon descends steeply among tea fields to the bridge at Tista. There it divides towards Kalimpong and Sikkim. On the continuation of the road to Darjeeling, the jeep free-wheeled for the last 6 or 7 kilometers, and finally we had arrived. Darjeeling is the main town of this region and its seat of administration. Actually, the name is Dorje-Ling, the place of immutable enlightenment, and it was the seat of Dorje Lama. The original Sikkimese-Tibetan settlement, now called Bhutia Basty, lies down the hill while the main town carries the imprint of the English colonialists. They came here during the rains each year to avoid the malaria in eastern India.

Darjeeling manifested in a dramatic way. A woman was throwing herself on the ground in the dark street and screaming wildly, bleeding from a wound on her head. We thought she had been robbed and bent to lift her up, but as we came closer, she just screamed louder. We saw that she was totally drunk and was screaming more from anger and spite than from fear or pain. As the disease would last no longer than her intoxication, we let her be. She was impressive, though, a natural for modern ballet or the opera.

The air was fresh, and even at night, the town seemed clearer and more magnificent than Kathmandu. It lacked the beautiful stupas and impressive culture, however. Also our cheap hotel did not have the charm of those in Nepal but neither did it have the dirt. Some buckets of warm water were a real luxury, and we had good strong dreams in the cold air.

Next morning, the outstanding Kanchenjunga range, with the world's third highest peak, sparkled in the sun. Darjeeling looked most inviting, and we found a path up from "Lower Bazaar," the poor part of town where we had slept, to the posh area above the main post office. It was striking how the large villas, shops, and restaurants there had preserved their provincial English atmosphere. Since cultures and languages tend to stagnate when leaving the living roots of their country of origin, many things here were more "English" than one could find in England today. General decay and a lack of well-paying tourists had created a crisis, however, and travelers of our kind, who don't want to be waited on and tend to look at the prices first were of little help.

Recently, with waves of rich Indian tourists now visiting town, service is once more in demand, especially coupled with the angel-like patience of the locals. It was much easier to satisfy the foreign empire builders than their own kind. The merchants from Bombay and Delhi who come to spend the money they hid from the tax-man are often exceedingly arrogant.

Breathing the clear, cool air, one agreed that Darjeeling is a health-resort. We were overjoyed to find stacks of letters from family and friends at the functioning post office. When heaps become embarrassingly vast in Nepal, they frequently burn them. Over the years, the town has remained an oasis of sanity in India. Despite its worn-down snobbishness, it simply has style.

The giant courthouse opened at ten. Here they issue the Sikkim permit. Arriving early, we meditated outside, invoking Karmapa's power that the permit be there. We had spent enough time in Asia to know that a notice in the central Himalayas was no proof that the information had actually arrived in the eastern part. To our immense joy it had, however, and we got the visas without difficulty.

The next necessity was a jeep. The ones for Sikkim left near our point of arrival. The stand was in lower Bazaar alongside the slaughterhouse, where coolies, taxi drivers, and woodchoppers live. The first stop was the pass at Ghoom. Going by daylight this time, we were glad to see stupas also in this area. Though childish in their execution and far from the intricate art of Buddhist Nepal, they were at least impressively situated on passes and hills. As the clouds drifting across the road lifted, there was even a moment's exciting view right into a Tibetan monastery.

Having turned left at Ghoom, the road soon descended steeply. From a height of 2,500 meters, it quickly falls to a few hundred meters. Here, a strategically important bridge crosses the broad Tista river rushing down from Tibet. Thus from the high air of Darjeeling, one descends again into what feels like tropical heat. The open slopes with tea bushes give way to banana plants with short, thick, triangular fruits, and mandarin trees which always look empty. These bananas are much tastier than the pulp-like things we get in Europe, and the inexpensive fruits felt good after the greasy food in the mountains.

Our data were written into a stately book at the bridge, an event which rarely takes less than half an hour. Thus our driver had time to find a few more passengers for his already hopelessly overloaded jeep. After wondering how they would ever protect the miserable suspension bridge against Chinese bombs or local Communist dynamite, the jeep rattled by the steep road up to Kalimpong on the right. Keeping the river on our left, we drove past a string of army camps. They were hidden in the forest but as usual not very impressive. After all, India was conquered by 5,000 English soldiers! Twice on each side of the bridge into Sikkim our papers were copied and checked. We were glad to supply so many people with really meaningful jobs!

After officially "dry" West Bengal, billboards here presented the local whiskeys as one of Sikkim's great contributions, probably in the field of chemical warfare! Westerners call their concoctions "monkey whiskey," and they are said to take both varnish and color from the table if one misses one's glass. There was even an alcohol-outlet called Karmapa, but we convinced the owner to remove the sign. The Tibetans could not read it, but it looked funny to Westerners.

It was great to see the first road signs in Tibetan letters, and here it fully dawned on us that we would now see Karmapa very soon. The passengers in the jeep probably had a few good stories to tell about the white giants who sat hand in hand with their meditation beads constantly moving, showing such enthusiasm for things which were completely ordinary to them. Their big subjects were the constant rain and their harvest.

About eight kilometers before Gangtok, the driver stopped suddenly at a broken down, narrow road branching off to the left. He pointed and said, "Up there is Rumtek, where the great Lama Karmapa lives." As we had masses of luggage, mainly gifts for others, and it was pouring rain, we offered him double pay to drive there, but having no license for this stretch, he did not dare. His advice was to sleep in Gangtok and return in the morning, when the weather was better. His words fell on deaf ears. Nothing could pull us even a step off the closest way to Karmapa. Having transformed ourselves into walking Christmas trees with our gear and gifts, an empty jeep came from the opposite direction. This driver was braver or did not have an uncle with a hotel. He was willing to risk the damaged road up to the monastery for thirty rupees. In the meantime, the rain had become like a waterfall. It was very unusual, and neither the jeep's canopy nor our umbrellas nor the plastic sheets lying around were of any use in keeping the water out. Relying more on memory than on sight, the driver slowly brought his party up 11 kilometers of winding road while even our best-protected articles had a thorough bath.

Suddenly, the headlights caught a gray-white wall with keyhole-shaped window-arrangements in dark colors. Then followed an open gate. This was Rumtek. It was late in the evening, and the monastery was already quiet. Nobody appeared on the stairs or while we put everything down in what looked like a waiting room. After knocking on several doors, we were greeted by some amazed-looking faces, some of them belonging to monks we knew from Kathmandu. They gathered and chatted, while others disappeared to find someone who spoke English. Eventually Jigmela came, a nephew of Karmapa who is today his official representative in Europe. He needed all his diplomacy to convince us that it was now too late to see "The Wish-Fulfilling Gem," as Tibetans call Karmapa. Finally, however, we were satisfied that meeting him the next morning would be more auspicious, and with relief, they made us a bed in the guest-house across from the monastery.

Rumtek Monastery

*H.H. the Karmapa
with some of his dogs*

In the morning, after half a year of deepest wishes, we finally saw Karmapa again. We came rushing in excitedly, and he caught us in his energy field, blessed us strongly, and said, "It's good that you have come; you can count on me as your teacher. Now, what do you want?" What we wanted was difficult to put into words. Actually, we had not thought about it. We said that we wanted to be with him and work for him, that he knew best what to do. "Okay," Karmapa said. "Tomorrow is full moon, a special day, when the retreat of the rains finishes. Tomorrow I will give you Genyen." We had no idea what Genyen meant, but coming from Karmapa, it could only be something good. We had our heads shaved, not knowing that this is only for monks and nuns, leaving only a few hairs near the whorl on the head. Sister Palmo, an elderly English nun, helped us get the traditional gifts we would need. She was an impressive lady of the old school who was able to stay for years at Rumtek due to an Indian citizenship. She had been with Dalai Lama first but then went to Karmapa because she would rather meditate than debate. At this time she did more for the Tibetan refugees and their culture than probably anyone else. Not everything was a success, however. Among other things, three of the four Tibetan incarnations she sent to Scotland in 1967, after training them at her school in the western Himalayas, became quite an embarrassment to Tibetan Buddhism. Especially in the UK and North America, they

Khechok Palmo, the English nun

seriously slowed—and slow—the development of a self-reliant Diamond Way Buddhism on transparent Western premises.

Hannah was charming beyond words. With the faultless white dome of her head shining in all directions, one could clearly see the intelligence inside. Also there was time to explore the marvels of the area while waiting excitedly for the next morning. Meditating whenever possible, we wanted to be open to Karmapa's gift.

Evening came early and soon most lights in the monastery disappeared. The growls of the long horns which followed assured the inhabitants of the valley that the protectors were there, watching over them. One window stayed lit, however. From Karmapa's room in the uppermost part of the building, it shone over the valley. When I woke up around midnight for a quick errand, the light was still there, and early in the morning, when excitement made it impossible to sleep on, it was still burning, although there were no other signs of life in the monastery. As we found out later, Karmapa rests his body at night but does not actually sleep. The ever present, all-pervading clarity of his mind is never clouded.

Even in the richly decorated upper meditation room, Karmapa shone powerfully. He sat on the floor behind a small table with his back to the window and received our gifts with a smile. Upon entering, some monks had shown us the traditional prostrations. One performs them by touching head, throat, and central chest with one's hands held together and then touching one's forehead against the floor. This is done three times. Until that moment, our democratic Western education had kept us from this symbolic opening and giving up of ego. We considered it something that natives in warm countries do but never imagined ourselves bowing to anyone or anything. Now, however, we did like the monks around us and bent down for the first time in front of Karmapa. It felt very strange at first, but our confidence in him made the unpleasant feeling disappear. Even the West adopted such bows to the lama or altar and that lasted until the mid-nineties. Then it became imperative to avoid any kind of outer ritual which looks similar to the practices of Islam.

Karmapa reached over the table and cut the last hairs from our heads. Thus he included us among those who practice Buddha's Teachings, frequently called Sangha. Then he gave us Dharma names. We had expected him to initiate us into some way-out meditation, to fly around in the sky, or produce some other very special event, but what followed was very different. During a nearly endless ceremony, we were expected to sit crouched on the floor in a most unpleasant position and repeat pieces of long Tibetan sentences after him. Soon our bones ached, but in his mighty presence, the question of the necessity of such an ordeal did not even arise. Then, at long last, Karmapa said, "When I snap my fingers, the Refuge comes to you. Concentrate." And actually at that moment, we felt something fall into us and knew that this was it. The monks chanted on, and Karmapa threw rice on us, but it was clear that the important thing had already happened. Finally, Karmapa said, "You must have confidence in me like in the Buddha." And we thought to ourselves, "We have even more confidence in you."

Outside on the roof of the monastery, the doctor translated our names. We surely could not complain. Hannah's was "Mighty Lotus Flower," and mine, "Ocean of Wisdom." The first part of the name, which all share, "Karma," means that one is in the Karma Kagyu-lineage of Diamond Way Buddhism. At the same time, it contains one's promise to use enlightened activity for the good of all beings. Actually, the meaning of the Refuge is limitless, and all its aspects are not fathomed until one becomes a Buddha oneself. Taking it with the motivation to benefit others, however, makes everything meaningful and part of one's development at once. After that, one's life has the taste of constantly recognizing new dimensions. This kind of Refuge is a meeting of compassionate truth-nature inside and out and goes much further than the "formal introduction into the Buddhist practices," as it is so often described.

In the process, one expresses one's confidence in the "Three Precious and Rare Ones," or the "Three Jewels": Buddha, his Teaching (Dharma), and one's stable friends on the way, the Bodhisattvas (Sangha). "Buddha" is beyond gods and men. The name represents the state of full enlightenment. In our historical period, it was first shown by the young prince, Sakyamuni, 2550 years ago. This state is everybody's indestructible, timeless essence even when one is unaware of it. His Teachings show what is relative and absolute and combine clear instructions with an active energy for realizing them. Also companions and helpers on one's way are important, otherwise most would do very little. Goal, way, and companions are thus essential to all schools of Buddhism. They bring hundreds of millions of people what is needed for a meaningful and independent life.

For walking, these three are enough, but whoever wants to fly also needs a teacher. His aware state is the students' contact with Buddha. He teaches what is useful here and now, and his activity supplies intelligent examples of how to benefit others. The Tibetan name for this fourth Refuge, indispensable on the quick and direct Diamond Way, is "Lama." It is represented either as a totality or as the union of three aspects. "Lama" here means the unbroken transmission of Buddha's blessings through a lineage of enlightened teachers, going all the way up to the present. Many experience it as warmth and joy, as a positive force one can easily trust. "Yidam" means mind's bond with enlightenment. It brings forth special qualities, worldly as well as spiritual. One's ability to identify with formed aspects of the Buddha-mind, be they peaceful, wrathful, female, male, single, or in union, is the key for working with enlightenment on this level. The beyond-personal impressions planted in the subconscious during a shared meditation or formal initiation grow and actively connect one to the wisdom of the Buddhas.

Actually these aspects, so famous from art-books and museums, are as real as one's mind. Wherever mind's open space plays freely, such pure forms and the corresponding mantra-vibrations occur. They emanate from the compassionate truth essence of Buddhas and Bodhisattvas to awaken beings' potential for enlightenment. Though countless skillful forms are known and used in Tibetan Buddhism, it is a mistake to be put off by their great number and diversity. They are pure expressions of one's mind, and all have the same essence. One only needs to realize one to get enlightened, the way that eating one dish may satisfy one. A good restaurant, however, has a long and varied menu.

The protectors, in Tibetan, *"Cheuchong,"* make it all possible. There are different kinds on different levels of realization, but the ones invoked in the Karma Kagyu lineage are all enlightened. They are Buddha energies that work with instant power for the good of beings. Their wrathful forms skillfully remove inner blocks and outer obstacles. In the above Lineage, the main protector is Black Coat, the great, two-armed Mahakala, and all other wrathful forms are active in his energy-field. Such forces are indispensable because of the great power of the methods used. Transforming inner neurosis as well as outer harmful influences on all levels and with countless means, the Diamond Way is no holiday. By activating one's deepest subconscious, it liberates material stored many lives ago. Thus impressions are set free which would normally not mature until old age, death, the stage after death, or in future existences. Now, provoked to ripen in a short span of years, such purifications of karma are not pleasant. Though joy and freedom actually deepen and increase, people are soft and have short memories. They easily lose courage when things are difficult, and thus a wisdom-energy is necessary to break and absorb their force, letting through only the experiences, which the student can learn from.

So, whether this fourth refuge is called "Lama" or "Lama-Yidam-Cheuchong," the meaning is the same. Its many dimensions become clearer, however, when using the longer formula.

As mentioned, the full meaning of the Refuge is only realized at enlightenment. Its strong positive influence, however, can be felt at once. It centers beings and connects them to the Buddhas. The meditations it empowers one to do, remove disturbing imprints in peoples' store-consciousness and dissolve much harmful karma. As Refuge makes one's mind function better, one will do more for others.

In Rumtek, the full moon of September is special to everyone. It is the end of the six-week "Yerne," or "Retreat of the Rains." During this time, especially monks and nuns make up for the missing practices during the year and meditate and recite early and late. This was the day for ceremonial dances. Early in the morning, we had already heard the growls of long horns and the insistent blare of oboes and had raced the few steps from the guest-house to the monastery to watch. In the main yard, enclosed by their cells, a procession of monks was doing three ceremonial rounds of the main building. They wore the traditional, broad golden-red hats of the Kagyu school, the original having been built around the shoe of the great yogi, Milarepa. Though clearly in their once-a-year best robes, however, there was none of the stiff self-consciousness which makes Western processions such a horror. Instead they laughed, joked a bit, and nodded at friends and family members who had come from everywhere to look at them.

The peace most feel near Lamas was even more pervasive than usual and touched everyone. The heavy smoke of burning juniper branches mixed with the creeping clouds which had been giving off rain nearly around the clock. Therefore it was only possible to see in glimpses. The monsoon was still on and would be extra unpleasant during the dances. Above a leveled-out rectangular plateau up the hill from the monastery, an enormous white tent roof showed the eight lucky signs. At its far side, a smaller tent had one side open. It offered an overview of the field, the roof of the monastery ,and occasionally beyond the valley, of the mountains of Tibet. After finishing their three rounds of the main building, the procession followed the stairs there. The high incarnate teachers took their seats in the small tent, while everybody else circled the dancing place and sat down. We found a place among the bigwigs, as close as possible to Karmapa. From there, one could often see his profile and hear his roaring bursts of laughter. Apparently originating in the very depth of his body, they rolled across the field again and again, easily reaching all. Among the many great Lamas we have had the chance to be with, Karmapa is unique in expressing the powerful joy of enlightenment. It is inseparable from him; his explosions of spontaneous happiness are irresistible, like the forces of nature.

Though the clouds looked like heavy rain, for some reason nothing happened. Then the dances began, supplying graphic inter-

The procession around Rumtek after "The Retreat of the Rains"

pretations of Buddha's teachings. The first play was by the young Shamar Rinpoche. He is senior among the young incarnates and an emanation of the Buddha of Limitless Light. Called *Opame* in Tibetan and *Amitabha* in Sanskrit, the Japanese know him as Amida Buddha and the Chinese as Amitofu. Shamar Rinpoche is a perfect example of how beyond-personal wisdom may influence one's choice of genes. He has similar facial features to the spontaneous representations of Amitabha Buddha, which have appeared in Buddhist cultures at different times.

The play dealt with the experiences of an untrained mind in the state called Bardo. This means the intermediate state between death and rebirth where one's consciousness is free of its old body and still hasn't attached itself to a new one. Until liberation, any mind is bound by its projections. Thus it experiences those processes as real, which are so thoroughly explained in the Bardo Thodol, the famous *Tibetan Book of the Dead.* Using symbolic acts and most expressive masks, Kunzig Shamarpa's play very graphically showed the maturation of subconscious material taking place after death. As already mentioned, when new sensory impressions are cut off at death, the untrained mind is no wiser than when embodied. It still sees its changing projections as real, and hate or pride, greed or jealousy, attachments or dumbness are the inevitable result. During not more than seven weeks, the strongest among these feelings structure one's perception and one finds oneself somewhere in the six conditioned realms. The experience of hells or heavens, as ghosts or demi-gods, in human or animal bodies are thus nothing but beings' stored actions or "Karma." One's experience of life and death consists of such changing dreams of passing from one existence to the next. In short, the play showed how conditioned states continue to arise until mind recognizes its open, clear, and limitless essence. Not until then are fearlessness, joy, and compassion unceasing, and their power beyond anything imaginable.

One really felt Kunzig Shamarpa reaching out to his audience. On the practical level, he combined absolute and relative teachings and brought goal and path very close together. For materialists, the impermanence and changeability of phenomena was stressed and for nihilists, causality. Showing how beneficial actions arise after death as friendly white appearances, while negative actions appear from that same clear space as black forms of fear and shock, the play was a good teaching for head tripping people of little maturity.

The next dance was age-old. It concerned a king who gave his possessions, his wife, even his eyes to others. He was surely generous, but the long stilted declamations made everything quite boring, and soon we were congratulating the queen on getting away. Actually, in spite of the folkloric ingredients, we were totally focused on Karmapa and what happened around him. He was simply more important.

Towards afternoon, we had to explain what we knew of Tibetan practices to a group of Italians on a luxury tour. It was strange how big and strong even southern Europeans look next to the central Tibetan and Nepalese races, but also how immature and individualized we appear. It was the first time I officially interpreted Tibetan religion and culture to Westerners, and it was a real flash, a first taste of that certainty and joyful excitement which would later become constant. The transmission worked, our deep interest turned them on, and all went to the tent to receive Karmapa's blessing. After that, nobody spoke, and most wonderful of all was the pleasure Karmapa and the other Lamas took in the process. Here, it became more than clear that they wanted to build bridges and be understood by the West. It was a realization that struck us like lightning and which we would not forget: a good-sized job to put in the center of one's life.

After the organized dances finished, and it still hadn't started raining, everybody else had their go. Spontaneously, and to everybody's amusement, they all showed their skills—wrestling, singing, or whatever. I was also asked to show a few tricks, and although at school, like most of my friends, I had been busy with more interesting things during physical education, all kinds of complicated jumps were in my bones, things the Tibetans had never seen before. They supported the stories, which had followed us from Nepal, and looking and behaving so much like the warriors from Eastern Tibet, again I was given the name of "Khampa." After that, it became impossible to avoid the limelight, and several times a day, I became the reluctant climbing tree for not very hygienic little monks or had to show the hardness of my well-nourished Western muscles. They were probably the easiest thing to praise, anyway.

At a pause between the dances, somebody brought a transistor radio, a gift of the Bhutanese king, to Karmapa. In 1970, it was a strange-looking thing in the Himalayas. They wanted it repaired. The way most Westerners think Tibetans have special meditative powers, which is not true at all, Tibetans expect "technical powers" from us. My Swiss knife was again useful, and all marveled at the wonder as it lay open. Though I much preferred the moving parts of motorcycles to radios and such little things, a loose wire fairly jumped into one's hand. It was on in a moment, and as the radio once again picked up the local thunderstorms; everybody was impressed. Hannah and I were also impressed. That whole day, while the rest of the valley was drowning, not a drop of rain fell on the area. Not until the plays were finished and everyone had reached shelter did the clouds burst, and then it poured for hours on end. The other two days of festivity followed the same pattern: just before the dances, the rain stopped, and right after finishing in the evening, it started again. On the evening of the third day, as casually as possible, I asked an English-speaking monk how this could be so. He simply replied, "The Wish-Fulfilling Gem (Karmapa) does not wish it to rain during the plays, and those monks over there are burning incense and saying mantras." It was not the last time with Karmapa that we wanted our school money back. Our formal education very much needed the liberating dimensions which Karmapa taught.

CHAPTER TEN

The Road to Bhutan

EVERY DAY, PEOPLE OF ALL KINDS came in droves to the monastery. They wanted blessings, advice, and an experience of Karmapa's timeless mind through the powerful Crown Ceremonies. The more his presence charged and purified us, the more their effect changed. First they were raw power, something physical, like being hit by lightning. I was shaken very strongly, and we were both left in a burnt-out but blissful and totally fulfilled state. Gradually, however, the experiences became more flowing, limitless, and enduring. Every ceremony brought new visits to states beyond time and space, and we raced to share in his mind at every opportunity.

Having managed to get to Karmapa, we did not want to leave again, and I had the bright idea of becoming his driver. Having learned on the great autobahn, I could move cars very quickly and unconventionally. At the back of our mind, we hoped that the Indians would not dare expel Karmapa's chauffeur. As a rule, foreigners are only permitted a few days in Sikkim, which is within easy range of the Chinese troops in Tibet.

While pulling whatever strings to be able to stay, at the same time our need for Karmapa's immediate presence gradually diminished. With his power-field so evident everywhere, we became less insistent on being near him always. Countless people wanted his attention, and he clearly had enough to do. With limitless kindness, he answered everyone's questions, solved their problems, and fulfilled their wishes. He did not avoid people many would write off as hopeless and did not seem to distinguish between productive and unproductive situations.

Upper stories of Rumtek Monastery

Seeing countless lives into the past and future, he apparently created bonds that would come alive at the right moment.

Through the daily Crown Ceremonies alone, Karmapa's blessing flowed constantly, and during this time, merely staying at Rumtek opened mind's potential. Hannah, however, soon felt that we should now get methods to move on. It was time to do a formal practice ourselves and not just enjoy the wonders offered. In response to our question, Karmapa ecstatically shouted three exceedingly powerful mantras. We should repeat them as much as we could. The first invokes his second incarnation in Tibet, the great yogi Karma Pakshi. Marco Polo claims to have met him in Mongolia and described how his magic powers humanized Kublai Khan. This mantra activates his energy field, and because he also was an emanation of Guru Rinpoche, it brings the additional blessing of the "old" (Nyingma or Dzogchen) school. The second was the key to Diamond Sow (Dorje Phamo). She represents the inner wisdom of all Buddhas, and already Milarepa meditated on her dancing female form, red, naked, luminous, and transparent. The third was the natural vibration of the often-mentioned protector, Black Coat, Bernak Chen, the active energy of the Karma Kagyu. In our amazement at not having such secret instructions whispered into our ears, Karmapa added the promise that these energy fields would now grow in and around us always.

A picture of monastic life at Rumtek gradually took form, with a typical day as follows: from around three in the morning, roughly their waking-time, the lamas and monks do their own meditations and recitations. At around six o'clock, they gather merrily at the washing place in the yard, which is often the only functioning water tap near and far. After that follows breakfast in their cells. It consists of Tibetan tea with butter and salt, mixed with crunched maize or rice. In Rumtek at that time, they received the only half-polished red Bhutanese rice from the generous King. Therefore, they were healthier than many of their colleagues subsisting on the fully polished local grain. Even so, about 80 percent had tuberculosis, and all were vitamin and protein-starved. When family members or supporters give monks money, they usually buy freshly roasted tsampa. It is their favorite food.

At seven, common recitations start in the main hall. Here, they pool their energies for the benefit of all beings or for a special family or individual. They activate liberating energies by focusing in unison on the texts and mantras of different Buddha aspects, and, as well as in deep meditation, the results are often very precise and appear with amazing speed. This process is called *puja* in Sanskrit and *cheupa* in Tibetan, meaning "invocation through offering." One distinguishes between outer, inner, and secret levels and the offering of space itself, but the real benefit is to oneself! By giving up the attachments of ego, one makes room for the Buddha's blessing. The use of music is here very conscious. The sounds resonate with the centers of awareness in the body and release mind from its constant preoccupation with sense-impressions and thoughts. The dissolving mental barriers allow a spontaneous joy to arise which is deeply purifying, and if one is able to live right into the music, strong inner experiences frequently appear.

During the noon break, another world of sound takes over. Now one hears the pitched voices of children learning to spell, while the older ones memorize different texts. It is no educator's dream of a modern learning process producing independence, understanding, and a rapid access to information. Tibetans definitely know better what to learn than how to teach it. However, what is learned by heart during these first years stabilized them. It is also the basis for their further education and gradually surfaces as a certainty, which helps them in life. Despite rampant sickness, frequent and brutal beatings by evil discipline-monks, and miserable outer conditions, they are more harmonious than children we have seen in other cultures.

In the afternoon, further pujas follow, or the monks take care of chores in and around the monastery. They print books by hand on wood blocks, page by page, make herbal medicines, or teach others. As dusk sets in and the long horns are again blown, they return to their private meditations, which the best of them continue during sleep.

When Karmapa visits, this daily routine comes totally off the hinges. Then visitors come constantly, ceremonies and initiations are given early and late, and it is impressive how Tibetans can improvise. Even when everything has been set up for a very special ceremony, they can accommodate any new developments without stiffness or hesitation. Somehow they can always change things so all feel that something special has been done for them. Years of meditation remove habitual thoughts, and they work very freely with the dimensions of time and space.

Hannah and I would have liked some more freedom, especially with time. Though inwardly set on a long stay with Karmapa, if possible for a lifetime, outer conditions did not agree. The telephone line from the Indian political officer, Mr. Das, glowed several times a day. He wanted us out of Sikkim at once. Until we came, no foreigners had remained in Sikkim for more than seven days, and after three days, one had to extend one's visa. Twenty kilometers north from the monastery along winding roads lies the Nathu-La pass to Tibet's Chumbi Valley. It is full to the brim with Chinese soldiers, and there had been skirmishes just a short time before. Actually, they could treat the Indians more or less as they wished, and this made the latter very edgy. The jovial English-speaking Dr. Jigme had already tried his influence with the authorities several times. He had informed them that Karmapa would now visit Bhutan very soon and that we would go with him. That had not changed anything, however.

Ourselves, we cared little about the authorities. If we stayed on, they could do nothing but throw us out, and they would have to find us first. But as guests of refugees with no legal rights and in a very vulnerable position with the Indians, much against our will, we had to do as they asked. It was very painful to leave Karmapa, even for a few days. We did not discover this opportunity to learn patience and observe our minds but instead burned with irritation at the Indian authorities, who had reached new levels of uselessness. As we took leave of Karmapa in his chamber on the roof, he invoked our compassion by saying, " They are acting out of ignorance by separating teacher and students. Such acts will bring later trouble. But they don't know any better." And with a twisted smile which went to the center of our hearts, he continued, "Take me as an example. I make wishes every day for Mao Tse Tung. He really needs help." Our agreement was to wait for Karmapa in Kalimpong and to drive one of his cars or trucks to Bhutan. There we would get Bhutanese passports, which need no visa for India and the Himalayas, and all obstacles to staying with Karmapa would be over.

At Rangpo, the border between Sikkim and India, the same officials sat around, and they were sour about our long stay. In those days war was a possibility, and they saw spies everywhere, as people so often do in countries where there is absolutely nothing to spy on. In the streaming rain, we did not cross the Tista bridge and check out of the restricted areas as they wanted. Instead, shortly before reaching it, we found a taxi for the narrow road winding up to the left, to Kalimpong. People always spoke of this town in a wistful voice. Up until the invasion of Tibet in 1959, Kalimpong had been the place where Tibet, Nepal, Sikkim, Bhutan, and India met to cheat each other in trade and politics. Although the Chinese had now closed off the important Nathu-La pass to Tibet, Kalimpong was still the place in the eastern Himalayas with the most things to be seen and heard, to be bought and experienced. Here also lived the Chinese yogi who for over 24 years had not moved more than seven steps from his house. When he arrived there, it was a nice residential place outside Kalimpong, but the town had exploded, and he now had hordes of noisy children on all sides. He managed to correspond with people all over the world and had sent the meditation on Liberatrice we used in Nepal. As it would be at least a day before Karmapa's caravan could possibly pass Kalimpong, there was time to go and visit him.

On the way through town, we dodged both Christian and Hindu missionaries doing a hard day's hard work. Imagine having religions that don't sell themselves! The yogi received us with many bows in front of his yellow house, and I recognized the environment from my gold run to Indonesia. It was the same ancient Chinese atmosphere as in Singapore, with masses of little pictures and artifacts everywhere.

The Chinese yogi was a small, round, and energetic gentleman of indefinite age. We later heard that he was then seventy years old. He told several unusual stories about finding his way to Buddhism in a Taoist society. At the same time, he darted with amazing speed around his workroom, collecting booklets from boxes and shelves everywhere. He had apparently written scores and now piled them in front of us. His communication, both written and spoken, at that time ruffled both our ex-hippie and recently "straightened" minds. The booklets frequently gave teachings on several levels at the same time, including much that is misunderstood by moralists and needs a lot of preparation and additional instruction. Also, until we assumed responsibility ourselves for the development of Diamond Way Buddhism, we were disturbed by his critical views of several well-known lamas. Not seeing the age-old politics behind the robes and smiling faces, we somehow thought that because the teachings were perfect, the teachers must be the same. Of course, Tibet was a medieval society and had neither known democracy, free voting, transparency, human rights, nor a press. In any case, with the known brutality of the surrounding countries and such glaring social inequalities inside Tibet, we should have expected the terrible punishments which took place there and a lot of other dirty laundry. So great is the power of idealized devotion, however, that while in the Himalayas, we hardly thought of the karma teachings as a tool to change things. To our relief, Karmapa was one teacher we never heard any gossip about. The mantra, "KARMAPA CHENNO" had once saved Yogi Chen's life as a giant dog had its teeth around his throat.

Most of this information was gleaned during later visits, however. At this first meeting, to us Yogi Chen was mainly the owner of the small but exquisite *thankas* on the wall. All were exquisitely made, many depicted fascinating Buddha-aspects we had never seen before, and their blessing sucked us in. He was also an expert storyteller, and gradually the picture became wider: At his birth, his mother had developed two extra nipples from which he had also been suckled. Apparently the deeper meaning of that was his receiving blessing from the four directions of the universe.

During his youth as a teacher in China, he had been disturbed by fears of premature death. He had spent years practicing the life-prolonging exercises of the Taoists but then picked up the Buddhist trail and went to Tibet to meditate. In Kham, he met with the famous French lady, Alexandra David-Neel. She was one of the first Westerners to travel the country and wrote some theosophically inspired books on very magical aspects of meditation. He did not mention the syphilis rampant in Tibet but stressed that she had not been willing to do union-practice with the yogis she visited in the mountains. He thought that it might have brought quick enlightenment to all and that this was quite a pity. He also told of his own years in a cave in Tibet, of the women who visited him, and deplored the present scarcity of "Dakinis"—women of awakened inner wisdom.

While still talking, and his English was quaint and interesting, he called a small boy from the group standing outside his window. They were gazing in the best Indian tradition at the strange man and his strange visitors. He gave some money and told him to fetch momos.

We knew momos well. They are the steam-boiled, chopped-up pieces of meat surrounded by dough which Tibetans love. Having been vegetarian for over three years—since the day the healing started—and wanting to stay that way, we told him in detail why we would not eat momos. So I called the child back and canceled the order, but again the yogi said something with "momo," and the boy ran off. We thought he had now ordered them with cheese inside instead of meat, which was also a possibility, but what arrived was clearly made from animals. As we once again and now emphatically told him that we were not going to eat meat, he answered that Buddha himself had eaten whatever was given. There was no way around the situation and down it went. We now expected a loss of blessing and all kinds of trouble. Especially we thought that the fear-hormones of the animal, which had surely not died in an ocean of peace, would reawaken my aggressive ways. Most of all, we wondered if the healing power of our silver bracelets would now be lost.

A few hours before the first healing in Copenhagen, inspired by Harald "the Prophet," we had left two pieces of ham on our plates. We would try not eating meat for a month. After the first "miracle" happened, we were sure there was a connection and had then simply decided to stay vegetarian. Also, we felt badly towards White Liberatrice, our special protectress. We were now eating the beings she blesses. To our surprise, however, eating the meat had no adverse effect on either body or mind, except perhaps that sleep was somewhat deeper and less conscious.

During the following weeks, we again avoided meat and even asked Karmapa for the vow to stay off it, but he would not give that. He clearly wanted us to be flexible. Today we do as most busy Buddhists everywhere: accept what is given and buy little meat ourselves. We never allow any animal to be slaughtered for our sake, which would make us a primary cause of the killing. One can help the minds of both animals and butchers by making good wishes for their future rebirths and by saying mantras like "OM AMI DEVA HRIH" over the food. If less than seven weeks have elapsed since the death of the animal, this is of great benefit.

In Kalimpong we stayed at the strategic and pleasant Gompus Hotel, overlooking all roads to and from town. The owner Tashi, his wife, and mother had connections all over the area. They would be the first to know when something happened. He was devoted to a 100-year-old Mongolian lama who lived on a hill above town and had special healing powers. We would have liked to visit him and also to see the local caves dedicated to the great Padma Sambhava, but Karmapa's cars were expected at any moment. So we hid from the police near the hotel entrance with packed-up rucksacks from morning on, ready to run out at once. Noon passed and nobody appeared. This was more than the usual Tibetan delay. Though there was hardly any chance of getting a call through to Sikkim, we tried and actually got the connection at once. Pulling the sun from the sky of our minds, Jigmela's clear voice confirmed a rumor we had heard early in the morning but had refused to believe: the road from Sikkim to Kalimpong had been washed down by the rain once again. To get to Bhutan at all, Karmapa had left during the night by the higher-lying military road. He might even have arrived by now.

That meant following Karmapa into Bhutan. It made no difference that is was a forbidden country to foreigners. As Karmapa's drivers, nobody would have stopped us at the border. Now we would have to trick the border guards ourselves, however, which could become exciting.

Some hair was again growing on our formerly bald and somewhat tanned skulls, and thus we did not look too different from the local

Khampas. Also, our traditional Tibetan coats, the so-called Chubas, masked our origin. The thing to be most careful about was not to show my blue eyes. They would bring trouble immediately. Entering the bus from Kalimpong to Phunchoeling, the first Bhutanese town on the way to Thimphu, the driver gave us a long funny look. Luckily, he was a Tibetan, and after a few words he promised not to tip off the border guard.

The upper military road went through picturesque mountains and run-down army encampments to a pass. Then it descended through vegetation, which somehow, in spite of the great humidity, looked like typical Mediterranean shrubbery. From there we entered the lowlands and drove east at a good speed. Keeping the foothills to the left, one passes through endless tea fields which are shaded by flat-topped acacia trees. At the first control post, we hid behind the seats in front of us. We had made sure to get places way back in the dark. It was a gift; the Indian officials just looked into the bus from the door and let it move on. The second control was less pleasant. Several customs people came into the bus, and one of them moved slowly along the aisle towards the back. We made ourselves as small as possible, kept our heads down, and pretended to be sick from the drive. I thought I felt the official's breath on my neck when he was next to our seat, but being more interested in the luggage rack above, in the murky light he did not notice our light-skinned heads. He turned around, the bus could go on, and with a triumphant feeling of really having made it, we rolled over the border into Bhutan.

It was now too late to travel up the mountains to Thimphu, the capital. No buses went at night, and there were seven control points on the way up. It would be smarter to spend the next morning in Phunchoeling getting the necessary papers. In this country, which showed such devotion to Karmapa and his teaching, we didn't mind abiding by the rules. I even had a dream of driving an official jeep up through the mountains to see how fast it could be done.

Actually, a night in one place wasn't such a bad idea. As we crossed the border, some strong karma had apparently matured. Hannah got very sick the moment it happened, so we found a room and hung our mosquito nets. In the middle of the night, Hannah saw a man going through our rucksacks. Apparently she had absorbed the teaching never to think badly about others deeply in her noble heart.

Instead of waking me, which would have brought a lot of action, she reproached herself for thinking that others would steal our things, considered it all a fever fantasy, and dozed off again.

The next morning half our things were on the floor, and the rest lay outside the window. Piling everything up, no equipment appeared to be missing. Even our trusty old Canon camera and several color films, very valuable in this area, were there. Only two things had disappeared, a photo of Karmapa with the Black Crown and a *thanka* of White Liberatrice, who is always so good to us. The photo was from OM studio at 11th mile in Kalimpong. We regularly bought that kind, sent them to friends, and used them as gifts. Losing the *thanka* was worse. It was somehow alive. White Liberatrice (Dolkar) is mind's female compassion, a perfect Buddha. Emanating from Loving Eyes, the principle of love, her power-field is very active in our time.

This white form of Liberatrice condenses out of limitless space with seven eyes. They signify both her receptivity to the sufferings of all beings and her ability to help from the level of highest wisdom. The extra eyes are on her forehead, on the palms of her hands, and the soles of her feet, which point upward in the lotus posture. Her right hand at her knee is in the gesture of compassionate giving, and the left hand at her heart holds the stem of a lotus flower. Opening at her ear, it signifies the original purity of whatever is.

The loss of this *thanka* was especially painful. Though simply and quickly executed: to a Westerner, its facial proportions were perfect. The old main painter of Rumtek monastery, a genius of form who was gradually going blind, was its source. Already now he was wearing two pairs of glasses on top of each other on his enormous head, and soon he would only have his inner vision and many disciples left. It was difficult to fathom this strange thief, secret policeman, or whatever, and we even felt that the pictures might have gone ahead to Karmapa in the mountains. Generally on the Diamond Way, such losses are seen as one's Buddhas warding off real trouble such as accidents or disease.

We asked our way to the local SDO, or maybe he was a DSO. We never wanted to get acquainted with the abbreviated titles people use in the former English colonies, trying to sound really pompous at the same time. Actually, it was quite understandable that they were important to those who lived from having them.

As it was still early morning, we went to his private house. We expected to share a good laugh at the way we had cheated the Indians and then to travel on with greetings to Karmapa and all the necessary papers, maybe even driving our own jeep. As his sleepy face appeared in the door of his bungalow, however, that was not his first offer. He looked as if he hoped he was still dreaming and exclaimed, "What on earth brings you here?" This S.D.O. looked typically Bengali-Indian, which we had not expected, but being inside Bhutanese territory, we explained that we were Karmapa's students, that we had missed him in Kalimpong, and that he had invited us to Thimphu. We would now like the necessary papers for crossing the checkpoints. Recovering from his first shock, he actually proved to be a kind man who would have liked to be of help. He had standing instructions, however, not to let anybody white into the mountains. They would have jailed us, he said, if we had been detected further up. Now he promised to get in contact with the authorities in Thimphu, not an easy task as the government would be on leave and attending Karmapa's ceremonies. Until everything was clear, we would be state guests in the rest house on the upper edge of town. They supplied a beautiful big room with a fine lawn and view of the hills and gave comforts of all kinds. Several Nepalese servants polished everything and fed us three good meals a day, more than we had given ourselves for years. Although we were living like rich people, however, our minds were rotating.

We felt inseparable from Karmapa's activity and knew that what happened in the mountains was important. Everyday he would certainly give very meaningful initiations in Thimphu while we were stuck in the lowlands, waiting for an invitation. Losing out on these ceremonies was all the more painful as we had begun to recognize their effects. Until then we had simply run from one to the next, enjoying the flash in the moment but not expecting a long time effect.

What is called "initiation," or *Wang* in Tibetan, means power and its transmission. Through a phase of focusing, with or without the use of ritual objects, a teacher activates an aspect of the unlimited Buddha-mind and passes it on to others. One can only transfer what

*At the
guest house
in Bhutan*

has been received through an unbroken lineage, and it is a great gift. As a result of initiations, one becomes able to experience both oneself and the world on ever higher levels until all action is spontaneous and effortless. No difference is then seen between the Buddha-aspect and oneself, and all things radiate in their timeless perfection.

During initiations, deep impressions are thus implanted in beings' subconscious, and a regular practice of Buddha's Diamond Way view, as well as the corresponding meditations, has frequently enabled beings to fully develop their minds. No joy equals that of feeling liberation and then approaching enlightenment. Even if it is difficult to work constructively with one's mind in this life, initiations are never wasted. During death and in future lives, impressions will reappear from one's subconscious. Manifesting then as powerful influences with the strength to turn one's karma, they bring about a rebirth where again one may meet with the Diamond Way. The energy-fields are thus active under all conditions and work step by step and life by life to bring their holders to full enlightenment. Therefore, there is much benefit in taking part in Buddhist ceremonies—also such that one does not understand—if one goes about it wisely. What one should not do, however, is to take initiations which are given with certain conditions if one is unable or does not intend to keep them. Also it brings confusion on deep levels to mix the initiation lineages of the different schools. Without thinking that other Buddhist transmissions are inferior, one should stick with the lineage where one feels at home.

So there we were, surrounded by the excellent service of our rest house, while happy natives passed through every day on their way to Karmapa in the mountains. We gave the travelers letters to him and the doctor and often tried to call the ministries in Thimphu. The government at that time had the staggering number of three telephones and no extensions. When we finally got through, it was to the Ministry for Tibetan Refugees, and before we could explain our wishes, the line went dead again.

Day by day we got more annoyed. Hannah was deeply unhappy, and I broke whatever came into my hands and reached unknown heights in black humor. Our egos just would not face the situation. Here we were, Karmapa's special and chosen disciples, sitting on the sidelines and wasting precious time. Clearly that was no problem to him. It was quite a fact to swallow. Also, starting the long walk up to Thimphu on a fine night, as was our frequent thought, was not possible. We had given both our word of honor and our passports to the D.S.O. After a week, he came to tell us that he could not keep us in Phunchoeling anymore. No answer seemed forthcoming, and we had to wait on in India.

Now what to do? We still had about twenty dollars but no visa for Sikkim, and we really did not feel like returning to Kathmandu. As we plodded out of Phunchoeling, overloaded and in a coal-black mood, the Indian border soldiers nearly broke their necks looking the other way. Officially they knew nothing about us, but even this we could not find funny. To shake the powers into action, which had helped us in hopeless situations before, I said, "Now we go straight to Denmark. This was enough." Of course, we did not want to go back. We had not achieved what we had come for. We still weren't established in a Buddhist practice which would guarantee constant growth. And worse: we had no clear direction, no way and goal to share with our waiting friends. Although we had been flashed out often by blessings, we knew we still hadn't changed fundamentally. The Danish championship in consciousness, which I so often explained as our goal, still hadn't been won.

But what were the possibilities? What else could we do but return to Copenhagen to make money, with little but a sack-full of good stories to pass on? While standing on the dusty road next to the border, a big luxury bus drove up, an unbelievable thing in these surroundings. It was full of rich French tourists, super-manicured in the latest fashion and tinkling with pop-art jewelry. On an excursion from Calcutta to the tea districts in Assam, they had wanted to also visit "chic" Bhutan. The Indians at the border, for whom Hannah and I had been exciting enough, totally freaked out at this invasion from another world. They shouted and aimed their guns at the bus in order to get the manifestation away, while I used the confusion to ask for a lift. Being nice people, they gladly took us along. It was quite a trip to suddenly be surrounded by well-functioning machinery and say civilized, meaningless things. We sat among oversized sunglasses, reflecting everything we had been brought up to strive for. As we got off several hours later at Siliguri train station, from where we could travel either to Delhi and home or up to Darjeeling, we knew one thing for sure—we were not going back to Europe. We could not just leave our Tibetans and Karmapa like that.

We expected mail in Darjeeling and also planned to write our parents. As we weren't making money by smuggling gold or hash anymore, they considered our stay in the East a time of study and would be glad to send us the money we needed. We would now ask for fifty dollars a month, not much for them but enough to be able to also share some with others. With luck, we could live on what we had left until it arrived. What drew us to Darjeeling most of all, however, was a rumor which had circulated at an all-night, open-air party near Swayambhu and which Hannah now remembered. In Sonada near Darjeeling lived a high old lama who, with Karmapa's permission, was the first Tibetan master to teach the traditional Diamond Way to Westerners. We had seen his picture fleetingly, and even through clouds of smoke, it had fascinated us. Now again his name came up: it was Kalu Rinpoche.

CHAPTER ELEVEN

Learning From Kalu Rinpoche

ARRIVING IN DARJEELING, we dressed in our one set of fine clothes, used only for special occasions, and went to get our student visas. The police in the Foreigner's Office, already sick of hippies then, were favorably impressed by my short hair and white shirt and by Hannah's beauty, so they let us apply. Due to the grinding bureaucracy in Delhi, this meant about six months of freedom before they even noticed we were there. After that, discovering that we were staying in the restricted areas with Tibetans and not spending money at one of their Hindu universities would take additional time. Finally, when the crunch came, we knew ways to delay being thrown out. Much time had thus been won for whatever we might want to do.

In a small clean pension by the post office, the rate was less than a dollar a day with breakfast. Very soon, however, it became evident that there were ghosts in the low wooden buildings. They were simply loaded with strange energies. During former editions of this book, we didn't want to influence the business of a kind but spiritualistic old lady who lives from renting rooms, nor did we find it right to wear out her spooks by making them tourist attractions. Now, however, 28 years later, so much must have changed that we can give the name of the place. It was Shamrock Lodge. It was not our impression that the ghosts or other energies were especially negative—they were mainly confused—but being very strong, they could be quite annoying. Several times in a row, they pushed books off the table under the nose of some very trustworthy acquaintances, piling the texts unceremoniously on the floor. Dr. Jigme from Rumtek, who once stayed for a week, ended up drinking himself to sleep every night. He felt the spirits constantly punching his back. Hannah and I were also affected, but only indirectly. Spooks know that I will jump right into any one that shows its sheet to see what they are made of. Their closeness produced a certain blankness and loss of blessing in the mornings, and a cool, sticky wind moved over my arms. Also, the blissful feeling of contact with Karmapa was weakened when they were around, which we strongly resented. Otherwise, all was fine, and the landlady talking to her black cats was quite a show.

While waiting for money and collecting information about Karmapa in these surroundings, the day came to visit Kalu Rinpoche. With an American friend, who had gone there before, we walked the entire way in splendid, crisp weather. On the first four miles up to Ghoom, the unbelievable Kanchenjunga mountains lay behind and to the right, and for the next five miles along the road leading to Siliguri, the lowlands of India were in front. Right before Sonada, we found his monastery. At about two kilometer's altitude, a group of shabby green-painted wooden houses lay up the hill to the left, across from a petrol pump. The first Tibetan on our way was Gyaltsen, a pleasant young monk who offered to bring our party to Kalu Rinpoche and also to translate. He led us into an oblong room with waist-high wooden paneling. There, on a bed behind a low wooden table on the far side of the room, sat an ascetic-looking man with a face few could ever forget. This was the high lama Kalu Rinpoche.

Although this frail old man hardly seemed present on a physical level, mentally he radiated a strong power. Also his outer appearance was an understatement. On several later occasions while driving him around Europe, he was tougher than his young Lamas. In the monsoon of 1983, at the age of eighty, he still gave two thousand initiations during a five-month period and remained active until he died in '89. We prostrated to him as was expected. Although it still didn't feel natural, we wanted to do honor to Rumtek and show good breeding. Kalu Rinpoche received us with a fine smile and gave us a strong blessing. Then he took out a school atlas of the world, and, as always in the warm countries, I impressively showed both Greenland and Denmark. With him, however, I was honest enough to add that the people live in the small green part and that the big white one was mainly ice. Also, I once more gave my version of the strength and

Kalu Rinpoche, first traditional lama sent by H.H. the Karmapa to the West, who has been especially active in France and Canada

toughness of the Danes. He had many questions about our Lamas in Nepal and Sikkim and especially wanted news of Karmapa. When he asked how long we wanted to stay, we thought for a moment and answered, "Until Karmapa comes back from Bhutan." "Good," he said. "You can stay here and learn with the others. This is my nephew Gyaltsen." And pointing to the young man who was translating, he went on, "He will help you find a room."

Outside again, Gyaltsen told us about Sue and Richard, Americans staying in a large old house some hundred meters up the hill and then to the right. There would surely be an extra room. At first, we weren't eager to settle in Sonada. The place had little charm. The monastery wasn't attractive, and the whole area lacked culture. It was defined by a single unkept road between rain-damaged wooden houses and stalls. In addition, it was very noisy. The miniature train blew its whistles every time it passed through, and everything seemed covered with a thin layer of coal dust. Sonada also lacked the addictive view of the Kanchenjunga range from Darjeeling, and lying before the pass, there was more rain and clouds. Worst of all was the distance from Mr. Singh and the only post office in the East that we trusted. On top of all this, the police didn't like people from the West to have too much contact with the Tibetans. They wanted tourists to behave like tourists, secretly imitated them when possible, and canceled extensions if one didn't fit into their view of the world. Kalu Rinpoche's suggestion stayed with us, however, and when we had our fill of nothing really happening on the level of learning and development in Darjeeling, we came south over the pass. For the sake of the authorities, however, our registration remained at the Shamrock.

Joining a handful of mainly Americans, Canadians, and French, a half-dozen resident and the rest passers-by, we came to the first teachings in Kalu Rinpoche's room. It was amazing that, except for the translator Gyaltsen, there were no Tibetans from his monastery or the neighboring refugee camp. Also there were no local Sherpas or Tamangs who could likewise understand his words. We hadn't yet become used to their mixture of complete confidence in the Dharma and amazing lack of interest in mastering it themselves. However, we knew with total certainty that such a tendency must never develop in the West.

Kalu Rinpoche taught about hell, about a whole row of hells. This was the last thing we had expected from him. Except for the lessons on Christianity in school when we had either done homework or been truant, Hannah and I had humanistic, not religious backgrounds. We were completely satisfied to be without funny gods or fears of a hell in which beings burned after death. We considered such teachings a mean trick to control weak people and empty their pockets.

What we expected from Kalu Rinpoche were deep psychological teachings, to watch him perform miracles or show signs of lightning-like enlightenment, and this was embarrassing. Here he sat in front of everybody and pointed to a large scroll with childish paintings. It showed figures being burned and cut apart and squashed between mountains, while others were freezing among giant blocks of ice. He told ghostly stories about eight "hot" and eight "cold" hells, about "neighboring hells," and a "sometimes hell." They had all varieties: in one, the customers, after having killed each other in different ways, were revived by a cold wind and then killed each other again, this circus continuing on and on. In other hells, they were put into big containers with molten metals or eaten by worms. One pain was worse and one hell more disgusting than the other, and Kalu Rinpoche claimed that one could easily fall into them if one didn't watch out. All this was heavy stuff; it was really too much! Western spiritual books were unanimous that one could not fall into the states of animal, ghost, or hell being if one had once reached the human level, that negative actions would only make one "freeze" on the same level before moving on. I told Kalu Rinpoche this, informed him that what the West had of spiritualists, theosophists, anthroposophists, and whatever all agreed on this view, but his answer was, "These are Buddha's teachings."

At that time we were still living in Darjeeling, and as we rode in a rattling jeep filled by carbon monoxide over the pass at Ghoom, we were discussing this old Lama. We agreed that these medieval stories, which fit better into a treatise on folk tales or manipulation through fear than in the high teachings of the enlightened Buddha, were quite exotic. Although we already knew that he could read our thoughts like an open book and probably was aware what was happening to us, we still thought, "Maybe he is getting a bit old."

The next day Sherab Tharchin translated. He was the offspring of an immensely rich American banking family and spoke excellent Tibetan. Apparently, he and Gyaltsen took turns. After hearing the teachings of the day before, we had checked the footnotes of the Evans-Wentz series again, our main source of information. Once more we were quite sure we didn't have to take heed of the hell-stories. We were fully willing to forgive the old man his mistaken stories of the previous day, if he would now only offer some interesting information. But again Kalu Rinpoche explained about hell; this time the subject was how they are experienced and how many years one has to spend in the different sufferings there. After a while, the lecture became a dry desert of astronomically high numbers.

The Americans, Canadians, and French who were clearly of less rebellious tempers were not so disturbed as Hannah and I. They sat there as docile as could be and simply wrote down everything he said while we were working up a steam. Although we liked this old warrior—he was from Kham in Eastern Tibet—and were taken in by his fantastic face and winning smile, we asked ourselves if these teachings were really for us. But we wanted to give him one more chance, and so the next day we went to Sonada again to hear what he now had to say. We could hardly believe it. The hells were still not exhausted. He now described which kinds of anger and what harmful actions, thoughts, and words take beings to the different ones. When on the fourth day he again started on the hells, I blew my top.

We really didn't come for the fun of it. Every day we had an hour-long journey from Darjeeling to Sonada and back. It was very unpleasant and took place in half-covered jeeps with about fifteen coughing people crouching inside or hanging outside. These were age-old Landrovers or Willis jeeps, built on commission from third-class materials. Their exhaust fumes from worn-down motors and third-rate oil made everybody sick, and there were stops for repairs on every trip. In return for the hardship and especially the daily expense to hear his teachings, we felt entitled to something attractive or at least meaningful. "We have already heard this before," I interrupted him. He looked at me with a fine ironic smile and answered, "That is true, but did you understand it?" Suddenly, we realized that we were missing his point. He was not speaking from the position of condoning that beings suffer. There was no judgment, pointing moralistic

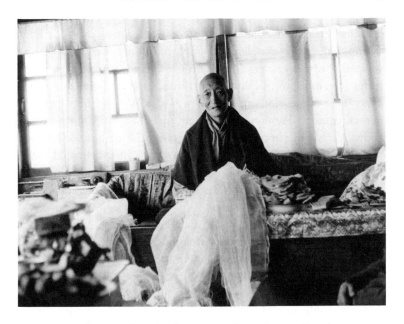

Kalu Rinpoche at his favorite seat for teaching at Sonada

fingers, or wish for retribution in what he had said. Also he didn't want to control anybody. His motivation for telling the incredible stories of suffering was only the best: He really believed what he said and told it to his listeners to keep them out of trouble. We, however, had developed irritation instead of compassion at his attempts and wanted to hear only pleasant things. This was no way to progress, and it struck us that the time of travels to exciting places and stray initiations was now over. A phase had come for thoroughly absorbing the teachings through constant and hard work with the mind. Right then, our habit of constantly moving made it much too easy to just absorb what one liked to hear, to grease one's false spirituality and self-made ideas, and avoid digging out the roots of ego.

A strong confidence in Kalu Rinpoche arose as a teacher who would not try to please our egos. Instead he would surely instruct us in what he felt was most effective and beneficial. So then and there we decided to move to Sonada and fully absorb his teachings. Now that we had removed our block towards him, also his hells became understandable. They were not the punishment of ill-natured gods but simply bad mental states, the outcome of former harmful activity. Through the many people we had helped out of horror trips, hadn't we seen how many strange things mind can consider real? How it can suffer even in its normal state while distracted by the myriad normal-izing sense-impressions of a human body? Weren't hells basically mental disease? Though we so rarely met their kind, didn't many beings already live in the hell of their own fears and doubts? In states which, like all conditioned experiences of the unenlightened mind, have no foundation or solidity? Though they are nothing but projec-tions, yet they are felt to be completely real and therefore bring suffering.

Now also the differences in views made sense: evidently the Western belief in the constant development of beings confuses two fields. One is the genetic advancement of the body—probably a fact until it was reversed at the beginning of the 20th century when natural selection fell away due to penicillin and machine guns. The other one is the perceived growth of mind's capacity. Actually, one's examination should start even earlier, with the process by which each being's illusion of a separate "I" takes rebirth. It should include mind's union at the moment of conception with the kind of body and environment which fits its subconscious contents. To make the whole picture even more complex, one needed the understanding that also in future lives unenlightened mind will continue to experi-ence as real whichever world its habitual tendencies and sensory apparatus now enable it to pick up. Thus, it is easy to see why Buddha advised so strongly against irrelevant speculation about karma.

This does not mean, however, that mind—the true essence of which is space and awareness—has the "form" of this body. That, therefore, as materialistic believers in reincarnation suppose, after the separation from one body, mind has to unite with another very similar one. Instead, as also explained in the *Tibetan Book of the Dead,* the process is more like Russian roulette. As sensory impressions fail after death, all minds' subconscious content comes alive. Then the stron-gest imprints and motivation gradually take the form of a dominant dream that pulls mind into the six realms of existence which best correspond to its content. This process is beginningless, like space, and until enlightenment, it is experienced as compulsory and full of suffering.

Thus, if impressions of pride are dominant, their maturation leads to rebirth in a God's realm. Those of jealousy bring one to the world of demigods, attachment, and varying amounts of good Karma produces a human life; stupidity sends one to an animal existence; greed to a ghost state; and hate and anger to one of the many hells that Kalu Rinpoche had just delighted us with. To a Buddha, all these processes are a dream. They are "empty" of any real essence and express the free play of mind's infinite possibilities. Seen from the level of purity, any phenomenon is spontaneously perfect—but to those caught in these states, they are never without pain. Even the greatest joy arising from conditioned causes is a weak shadow of the bliss that is mind's constant and true nature. Moreover, most beings regularly miss out on even their conditioned joys.

There was a room in the so-called Crees house, up the hill from Sonada—an enormous wooden building in Tudor style, which had been built by an Italian millionaire. He wanted to cure his tuberculosis in the high altitude but had died before even seeing it. Now the young Nepali widow of an English pastor lived there, surrounded by two or three worlds. In the lower story and the huts around, her countless relatives all lived in traditional Nepalese style. In these extended families, where everybody calls each other brother or sister beyond the suckling age, it was not easy to see which child belonged to which mother. If they had any check on the fathers, often Gurkha-soldiers coming on leave, we never found out. Anyway, on the ground floor everybody was noisily all over the place all the time. Then there was her son by the priest, a rock musician whose dressing and thinking, with the inevitable Indian delay, followed the fads in Europe. Finally, occupying most of the upper story, was our unusual strange group of Western mantra mumblers.

In the meantime, the first 150 dollars from my parents had arrived. The bank would only give six rupees for a dollar, the free market in Darjeeling nine, but Calcutta paid a luxurious 12. So we made the first of our quick Calcutta-and-back trips, using the dependable night trains to save time. These one-day tours, a regular event during the many months ahead, actually became an important practical supplement to the teachings. Coming from the serenity surrounding Kalu Rinpoche to the overwhelming problems of this endless slum of a town, the pain of the conditioned world was especially visible. Back at the teachings again, we could only agree: "It really is like that. Those things are going on. We just saw those conditions ourselves."

Timing the trip as well as possible, we left at the end of the "hells," stayed away during a few ceremonies, and made it back for the "hungry ghosts" and "animals." Hungry ghosts are beings in states of extreme greed and attachment. Their mental processes are totally dominated by avarice: they constantly try to get things and hold on to them. But as nothing can be ultimately "had" or "kept," they are in constant frustration. Their intense tightness focuses on things to eat and drink and distorts their perception. To many, food changes into dirt and fire as they come near it, while others experience the illusion of trying to fill town-sized bellies through throats and mouths having the size of needle-eyes. A lot of the descriptions matched paintings by Bosch and Breugel. Rinpoche's teaching on ghosts was very effective. Up till today, it added an automatic "Is this necessary?" to any arising material wishes.

An "animal" birth springs from ignorance, from distorting things consciously, or not using mind's potential. The main suffering of domestic animals are their slavery and slaughter by humans. Those in nature hunt, harm, and eat each other. Most live below the earth or in the water. They have no ability to control their minds, no chance to work towards any kind of liberation. These three—hells, ghost-states, and animal realms—are called the "lower" worlds. They are the natural maturation of mind's negative impressions, and it is only common sense to avoid planting seeds that will bring forth such miserable results. There really is nothing worth looking for in these states; they bind one totally, and there is no opportunity to help either oneself or others.

"Also the upper worlds, the 'good' rebirths, have suffering," Rinpoche told us next. "They are no certain refuge." When predominant desire and good actions from former lives take one to a human birth, these eight sufferings are automatic: the four evident ones of birth, old age, sickness, and death, and also four sneaky ones. These are the pain of being separated from what one likes, the frustration of being with what one doesn't like, the suffering of not obtaining what one wants, and the trouble of having to guard what one has. He described each one in the minutest detail, showing how so much of what is considered "natural" is really unsatisfactory or disguised pain. "Gods and demi-gods are not to be envied, either," he said. Demi-gods are born with beautiful bodies and power because of former good actions, but their strong jealousy fills their lives with fighting and intrigue. They are never satisfied, and as they usually die in states of great anger and hatred, their next rebirth becomes extremely painful.

The Tibetan Wheel of Life

Even the most joyful states in the conditioned world, those of "gods," offer no lasting satisfaction, as the illusion of a separate "I" is still intact. Although for eons of time one may here stay in states of extreme pleasure, experiencing the automatic fulfillment of wishes, worlds of pure form, and the freedom of total abstraction, it is not a permanent state. Nothing can keep the accumulated good karma, which causes the experiences, from finally becoming exhausted, and one then falls into lesser levels of experience.

It is the same in all realms. Until highest, joyful Buddha-wisdom has removed dualistic thought-patterns due to inherent ignorance, mind experiences its emptiness or space-nature as a "me." This makes what appears in it, its "clarity," into an object or a "you." The illusion that the experiencer and the thing experienced be separate produces desire for what one likes and ill will towards what one dislikes. Desire naturally leads to greed, as one wants to keep what is pleasant, while aversion causes envy: one doesn't want one's enemies to do well. Finally stupidity causes the useless kind of pride that makes one feel to be better than others with the resultant loneliness and stiffness. Identifying with what is impermanent, such as thoughts, body, and wealth, blocks mind's experience of its boundless radiant space, and suddenly, even the gods have fallen. Such disturbing feelings bring about harmful words and actions, and their inevitable effect is the suffering and dissatisfaction of beings.

This mess, which most cannot control or ignore, is experienced as "life," on whatever level of existence it occurs. Using very practical examples, Kalu Rinpoche showed how duality strikes on each of the six conditioned levels and even among the highest gods. "Only one state," he repeated insistently, "is eternal and perfect: that of Buddhahood." Only one goal, he taught us, is really worth pursuing! That of reaching a level where one's own veils are gone, and the will and power to work for others have fully matured.

After this week-long obstacle course through the poor bargains of conditioned existence, the direction of the teachings changed. Kalu Rinpoche now switched to telling his listeners what a singularly lucky existence they presently enjoyed. How, among the countless beings filling the universes, they had obtained the precious opportunity for practicing Buddha's teachings and becoming free. "Eighteen conditions came together for this situation to arise," he said. "Eight 'restless' kinds of existence had to be avoided, while five conditions were obtained from others, and five come from yourselves." He enumerated them all and went on, "All of these are active here and now, and offer you a unique opportunity."

Removing the veils of ignorance and disturbing feelings became something close and relevant under his guidance, something many felt they could do. The perfection he described was no dream either, but mind's true, changeless essence which one is never without. Making perfection very real, he inspired even the laziest members of the group, and his next teachings on impermanence added urgency to the former ones. Pointing out the fleeting nature of all things, the certainty of death, and the shortness of life, he made everybody conscious of the many signs of change and decay everywhere. "In this life you have the chance to find that which cannot die or disappear, your own Buddha nature," he said. "It is a precious opportunity, but life is short. If you don't use it now, how many lives of pain and confusion will you go through, unable to help others or yourselves, until again you meet these conditions to become free?"

Even with our new-found good will towards the teachings, Hannah and I had real difficulties incorporating the phenomenon of suffering. My mind recognizes pain and frustration as flawed programs and kicks them out, and nobody in the Sonada group seemed to realize that the view expressed was from a Buddha's level. In the traditional way it was presented, it had little relevance to us. Being the happiest people we know and feeling all things to be meaningful and exciting, it was not a whip behind but an ever-increasing carrot in front which motivated our practice. That even the highest and most joyful states we know now are but a weak shadow of the limitless bliss of full enlightenment would have been a much stronger incentive.

That was to come later, when I gave those teachings myself. Kalu Rinpoche left the subject like this: "Three kinds of suffering are inherent in all conditioned existence:

1. The suffering of suffering, that state where the accumulation of pain becomes unbearable.
2. The suffering of change, that whatever appears will also disappear.
3. The subtle suffering of ignorance, due to not knowing what is really going on. Only Buddhahood is totally beyond these faults."

CHAPTER TWELVE

Karmapa Sets the Course

In the Crees house, our American neighbors Sue and Richard spent hours doing a strange kind of gymnastics. They touched the top of their heads, their throats, and then their chests with their hands pressed together, as we had learned during refuge. But instead of touching their foreheads to the ground in a ceremonial way, they slid forward on their hands until their bodies were stretched out to their full length on the floor. Not resting even for a moment, they then got up again, repeating the process many times. A Canadian called Ken performed them dramatically during the pujas in the monastery hall, while others did them at home. Maybe we had stepped on some devoted students' toes by being so adamantly for Karmapa or putting challenging questions to Rinpoche, or we did not know how to ask in the right way; anyway, everybody seemed too busy with their own practice to tell others what they were doing, and information was difficult to obtain. So we forgot about the practice even though I felt intrigued by its athletic aspect. Not until the end of his teachings on suffering did Kalu Rinpoche explain the gymnastics we saw the others doing.

Apparently 100,000 such "prostrations" were the first of four foundation practices. The masters of the authentic Tibetan Buddhist Diamond Way have always claimed that success with simple practices like Shine, Lhagtong (Shamatha, Vipashyana), as well as really advanced "Tantric" meditations, is largely dependent on such preparations. They can only bring true results after the intense accumulation of positivity and wisdom brought about by such preliminaries. In addition to effectively removing pride, the prostrations exert a very powerful influence on body, speech, and mind. They straighten the energy channel in the middle of the body and turn one's mind towards enlightenment. "The hundred thousand prostrations are the first decisive step on the way to enlightenment," Kalu Rinpoche often said. And although they are called The Hundred Thousand, or *Bum* in Tibetan, one actually had to do them 111,111 times.

Hannah was ready to start right off, but my pride smelled the danger and quickly found a way around the challenge: "If he wished us to do them, Karmapa would already have told us. And if we start, we should finish all in a stretch. It is better to just meditate until we are with Karmapa again." It was a smug way of avoiding them. Even if we did a thousand a day, they would take over three months, and we definitely didn't want to stay in boring Sonada that long. We were still totally tuned into Karmapa, and though we were happy to have Kalu Rinpoche for a teacher and felt our thankfulness growing daily, there were whole layers of devotion which were open only to Karmapa, to the great laughing Buddha in our hearts.

It wasn't easy to see others doing prostrations without trying them myself, however. So one day, driven mainly by curiosity, I cleared some boards on the floor of our room. Placing a sleeping bag as knee protector, a cushion for the stomach, and a pair of worn-through socks for the hands to slide on, I wanted a good go at them. Considering it a one-time test, I would just try them out and tell no one about it. They brought a special feeling, actually an exciting one. At 17, when I had been in the U.S. on an A.F.S. exchange program, the flying tackles in football had always given me great pleasure, and here I found the same high, speedy feeling again. The one-pointed-ness of the motions was addictive, and I probably did 500-600 without stop. That was all I wanted to know about their effect, and, except for my aching stomach muscles, I filed prostrations under exotic sports. As we came to the next teaching, however, Kalu Rinpoche put on his loveliest of smiles and said, "It's very good that you have started the prostrations. They are very helpful in removing all negative impressions from body, speech, and mind." He praised me highly, and some Tibetans present picked up the lead and loudly confirmed the usefulness of the 100,000 prostrations. It was embarrassing. It would be total sabotage to state in front of our hopeful group that I had only conducted an experiment and had no intention to continue. It would have stopped others in their practice, also, and harmed Rinpoche's work. There was no way out. We had been expertly fooled, and Hannah and I started doing 200, three times a day. It left us enough time to also do many other things, like checking out those interesting Himalayan foothills that lie between Nepal and Bhutan and border on Sikkim.

People said that Kalu Rinpoche was not the only high yogi around Darjeeling. On the wood-covered slopes above town lived a teacher called Kanjur Rinpoche. He was a disciple of Karmapa from Tibet and one of the highest teachers of the Nyingma lineage. Although Hannah and I have always had the good instinct of staying with one lineage and not mixing the teachings (it's better to not understand one thing than to be very confused about several), we were still curious and blessing-hungry. So one day we went on the beautiful walk through the woods to visit this master.

Though much of the terminology is different, during the centuries, the teachings and blessings of the Nyingma school have mixed with those of the Kagyu lineage several times. They are now an important part of our transmission. Often both lineages are held by one lama at the same time, and in his third incarnation as Rangjung Dorje, Karmapa saved their highest wisdom of mind, called Great Perfection or Dzogchen, incorporating it into the Kagyu Great Seal or Mahamudra-stream. Generally one can describe Dzogchen as most useful for people with anger, and Chagchen as the way of those with dominant desire. For those who trust their inherent Buddha-mind, both are the quickest way to the goal. Kanjur Rinpoche lived with his wife and incarnate son on a hillside with large juniper trees. Their big, beautiful cement house was under construction, and they were surrounded by a group of exceedingly wealthy French disciples. To get in, we first had to open a gate guarded by a pair of noisy German shepherds. They were in a bad mood, and a few days ago, the French said, they had chewed somebody up. None of the Westerners sitting around, however, seemed interested in being useful to newcomers. Like several of those closest to Kalu Rinpoche, they were apparently too occupied with their own development. We promised ourselves once again that whenever we started making Tibetan centers in the West, anybody creating a sour atmosphere would be kicked out.

Especially I did not forget that vow later, and it is an activity that I
actually enjoy. Bureaucracy, surliness, and egotism the Diamond
Way just cannot afford; they completely betray Karmapa's spirit.

The dogs wanted no trouble when we managed to open the gate,
and Kanjur Rinpoche appeared at once. He was touching, marching
ahead into his house in slippers and a long nightshirt. His wife also
had a loving vibration, and it was impossible not to like them at once.
Rinpoche sat down on his throne, asked a few questions, and then
went into meditation. We meditated along with him as well as we
could and, suddenly, that meant a lot better than usual. We were in
mind's essence, beyond thoughts, at the same time totally gone and
totally clear. As we returned to daily consciousness with ideas and
discrimination, some hours had passed, and getting on the late bus
back to Sonada, his blessing was still there. On a later visit, something
similar happened. Sitting down on a chair in front of us, he started
chanting, "OM AH HUNG BENZA GURU PEMA SIDDHI
HUNG." Suddenly the inner energies moved upwards so strongly
that I shook all over, feeling countless dimensions open up. Full of joy
and gratitude, I leaned my forehead against his knee. He died while
we were with the Rumtek-party in Geneva in spring 1977, and at that
time, Karmapa promised that he would take rebirth soon. A few days
before ending his own 16th incarnation in Chicago in November
1981, Karmapa confirmed Kanjur Rinpoche's new one as well as
those of 20 other important lamas. In Tibet, Kanjur Rinpoche had
first been one of Karmapa's monks. Meditating very strongly, a
wisdom-holding woman had come to him, and he reached non-dual
levels of awareness.

Chagdral Rinpoche, another high lama of the Nyingma school,
was also worth visiting. Near Ghoom, his monastery is a landmark
because of its beautiful stupas in the old Khadampa style. He is no
incarnation, but reached his level of consciousness in this life. A close
friend of Kalu Rinpoche, he is famous both for his divinations, which
draw many people, and for his hard, practical teachings. Once he
made a Western groupie-type girl clean a stable for half a year, and she
came down with T.B. before she received any teachings from him.
When he gets money, he often travels down the hill to Siliguri. There
he buys the live fish he can afford, says mantras over them, and puts
them back into the river. He's a vegetarian, and like all disciples of

Guru Rinpoche, he considers smoke harmful in any form except for incense. "It keeps the Buddhas away," they say. Concerning alcohol, however, they have a wider view. Taken with control, it's even supposed to prolong life. In Tibet, he visited many caves where Guru Rinpoche and Milarepa had left their blessings. One donkey carried his books and another his food, and he meditated as he liked. Shortly after, the very generous Bhutanese royal family helped him start a retreat center in Nepal. When we saw him last in the autumn of 1981, he was doing fine.

The head of the Nyingma school was then Dujom Rinpoche. He died in France in 1987. Like Karmapa, he was constantly surrounded by supporters and people seeking his help. He moved between Kalimpong and Kathmandu, and during the seventies and eighties, he taught in the West several times. Especially in London, Paris, and New York, groups appeared under his guidance. We had already tried to visit him in Kalimpong, but the house was deserted. Now in Darjeeling, we just managed to see him the day before he left. Dujom Rinpoche suffered from very heavy asthma. His students considered it a sign that he took on the bad karma of many beings, while Yogi Chen quoted his Taoist sources and claimed that he made love too often! Whatever people thought, Dujom Rinpoche's weakness gave many people good karma from being useful to him. He stopped our prostrations, and as we asked how he was doing, he answered so simply and matter-of-factly that a whole world of clarity appeared: "I'm miserable." He gave us packages of "Lama medicine," small irregular grains of herbs that are blessed by yogis and lamas during week-long invocations, and ended with a very fine, light blessing. On our third pilgrimage in 1981, he still managed to bless our hundred friends.

On the mountain slope between Darjeeling and Ghoom, also up from a petrol pump, lived the Drukchen and the Thugtse Rinpoches. The former is now here in a new body. They had little love for Kalu Rinpoche, who had apparently bought Sonada under their noses. A major contribution of theirs to the area were large courses and collective recitations. Through them the local Buddhists were brought out of their traditional "consuming" roles and made to be active in their own lives. The architecture of the monastic building was advanced, and the puja had amazing beat, but we were quite disturbed to see a certified Tulku who had gone mad. There was no room for that in our understanding then.

A place of frequent visits became the Bhutia Basty community, which lay behind Darjeeling. It was interesting because it functioned as a lay organization, but they still had a lot to learn! Their collective group processes were much less productive and transparent than what became possible in our Western groups later.

These visits to neighboring lamas, however, did not make us forget that Kalu Rinpoche was the one to learn our methods from. If it didn't happen indirectly, as in our case, Karmapa frequently sent disciples to him directly so they could learn their Buddhist basics. Still today the traditional teachings and celibate hierarchies from his ancient Tibetan monastery form the backbone of his French, Canadian, Norwegian, and U.S. monasteries, and the practice is in Tibetan. In the more than 200 lay and yogi centers we and our friends have established directly for Karmapa till 1998, however, especially Kunzig Shamarpa's activity has added important conceptual material to this structure. The groups work on the level of friendship and themselves decide on matters of organization. This open approach, the frequent teachings of Great Seal (Mahamudra), and the wide use of meditation on the teacher (Karmapa) and in one's own language has brought amazing maturity to many. The fact that the latter groups are lay and transparent makes them a part of life and produces an open and level playing field for the brightest and most independent minds.

Although we learned from Kalu Rinpoche nearly every day and did our prostrations under his guidance, we still wouldn't take initiations from him. They touch mind on levels where we wanted nobody but Karmapa. Once we left his room just before an initiation, and all felt strange about it. Kalu Rinpoche saw the squeeze we were in, and one day he said that Karmapa would soon be going from the eastern to the western part of Bhutan. He would have to pass through India to do that, and we should use this opportunity to ask him about the initiations. That was the best we had ever heard from him! We jumped in the air with joy and excitement. It was beyond wonderful. The idea of seeing Karmapa again made everything radiate, and during the next few days we gathered information about his route and the police presence in the area. Though we could rarely discover which channels the news traveled, some of the warrior-type Khampas everywhere always knew what Karmapa was doing. They said that in the course of the next few days he would travel a stretch through India. This was necessary because the direct road connecting the two sides of Bhutan had not been completed. As there was only one road, we could meet him where we had entered the luxury-bus. Without difficulty, we picked up the papers for Kalimpong. We were glad to know the military road from there. Because it was only used when the main one had fallen down, all the way to the Bhutanese border there were no further controls.

This time we got off the bus before the gate, went to the border post, and asked if we could wait there for Karmapa. The officials weren't the same geniuses as last time, but they were just as paranoid and threatened to arrest us if we didn't go away quickly. They were probably afraid of losing their jobs, and in India that is not joke. We told their chief that we were Karmapa's students, but he didn't believe us. Apparently, he had some classic Hindu education and kept repeating, "Such a strong karmic bond you don't get in one life." Of course, it sounded strange that a pair of blond Europeans should feel like closest family to the highly honored Karmapa, teacher of the greatest Tibetan yogis and a growing number of Indians. What the guard's philosophy missed out on, however, was the possibility that many of the big-boned people with white faces who now explored the East must have lived there in earlier lives. Just as those Asians who feel drawn towards Christianity, and not only for the money and higher caste involved, were surely collecting impressions in Christian cultures before.

Actually, recognizing one's students, at least by their general characteristics, is not difficult. However, one should rarely say anything about former existences. People start speculating; it is difficult to be really certain, and most already have enough trouble with their egos from this life. It is better to avoid a lot of personal drama, and just continue teaching where the best potential exists.

The border officer showed no gratitude for this enrichment of his philosophy, and since it was both a waste of time and could lead to a big mess—they were quite desperate—we put our rucksacks back on and turned around. After a short walk along a sandy road bordered by gnarled pines, a Bhutanese jeep picked us up. It took us to the next village, which was still inside the restricted area. As no other roads crossed or entered the one we were on, Karmapa would have to pass by this way. There would be no need to go anywhere else. We quickly moved off the main street to avoid any police, secret or in uniform, and started looking for a place for the night. In addition to being free of nosy authorities, at the same time the little town was the most pleasant place we had come across south of the Himalayas. Inhabited by natural and gentle people, it lay in the shade of enormous acacia trees. It was a relief to be around Indians with whom one didn't have to be educational. When we asked where to find a hotel, they took us directly to the main temple, spread out a mat, and invited us to stay. It was like before the waves of hippies hit the East. There was even a functioning telephone in this paradise, and when we heard from Phunchoeling that Karmapa would not come until the next day, their hospitality was right on.

Our mat lay next to the main shrine, and at intervals, the local people came in. They struck the gong to wake up their god, offered the food or coins they brought, made their wishes, and left. Some also brought us food, and shortly after, members of the Tamang tribe, who are mainly Buddhist, invited us to bless their temple. It was a situation where a single act would say very much. Would we collect out gear and take it along, or would we trust them? For the first and only time in India we decided to risk leaving it, and as we walked off, talking only what we always had in our pockets anyway, we felt that they were glad.

The Tamangs took us up a shadowy road under newly planted trees, and we thought, "This is how beautiful India must have been before the white man gave them penicillin without contraceptives and the population exploded." The temple was not far from the village. It was built on poles to keep snakes and rats out, and the Tamang-style was unmistakable. Like everywhere in the foothills and here in the plains, one saw the white, four-armed *thankas* of Loving Eyes with extra large hands and eyes. Next to them were the same unfinished looking dorjes and bells made by the local smiths. They used simple molds and couldn't heat the metal enough to get the impurities out.

Apparently they didn't use the temple very often, and we had the feeling that much of their practice would be quite "wet," involving lots of alcohol. Still the fundamentally good energies could be felt that appear wherever people even think of the Buddhas. We blessed the place with the mantras we used and threw rice.

The next morning we chose a strategic position which gave a wide view of the road without making us visible. In addition, speed-breakers and the entry into the village would slow down the procession. Some hours and a dozen bananas later, Karmapa arrived in an open Landrover at the head of his convoy. We ran in front of his jeep, and he made the amazed driver stop. Talking and laughing a lot, he took his time to thoroughly bless us.

A moment later he gave orders to have us hidden among the luggage on top of a truck, and suddenly we were once again in Bhutan.

In Phunchoeling, the cars stopped at the guest house near our former rest house. We dodged lots of Rumtek friends who wanted to chat and ran straight to Karmapa. Hardly noticing the line of dignitaries waiting to enter, we raced in at once. This was the moment for giving him our Danish passports and getting Bhutanese ones instead so we would not have to leave him again. The thought of ever returning to Europe wasn't even in our minds; we just wanted to be close to him. As he held them in his hands, Karmapa said, "You are lucky to have a country and not be refugees; you should know that. Keep them; they will be useful later." Promising that he would do what he could, he invited us to sit on some bamboo chairs next to him.

Something felt strange. It was somehow not possible to get comfortable in the chairs although we were too occupied with our plans to understand why. But as a strongly built man whose face we knew from buttons on many lapels and photos everywhere stepped into the room and sat down on the floor in front of Karmapa, as inconspicuously as possible we slid the same way. It was the King of Bhutan himself.

Late that night it became possible to see Karmapa once again. As we stepped into the room, we nearly fell out again with surprise. It contained no outer source of light, yet it was illuminated by a golden radiance with what looked to me like a slight tinge of green. This light came from Karmapa himself. When we recovered enough to speak, we asked first about the initiations. Karmapa smiled, "You fat-heads. Can't you see that Kalu Rinpoche does my work? Of course you should take initiations from him. Go back to Sonada and do the foundation practices. Then come visit me in Sikkim whenever you can."

We also met the Royal Family. In 1979 and 1987 they kindly invited us to Bhutan as their guests. The King is now married to Chechoo Rinpoche's four nieces. Also, Jigmela, Karmapa's nephew, was there and made a point of telling us how quickly people in retreat finish their prostrations. After a last Crown Ceremony for the hordes of spaced-out looking hill people who had come, we were off again at three in the morning. This time transportation meant a soft seat in the cabin of a truck, next to our old friend the doctor. As Karmapa had more stops than we did, blessing people and places, the truck arrived at the Tista Bridge first. There we waited with the pictures and objects which hadn't been blessed in the great rush, things we would send to our friends at home. Blowing on the stash in my hands while his jeep crept past, suddenly he was over the bridge.

CHAPTER THIRTEEN

Home in Sonada

FROM TISTA WE TOOK A SERVICE JEEP bound for Darjeeling, got out at Ghoom, and found a truck down to Sonada. Now, for the first time, we belonged there. Karmapa wanted us to stay and learn, so that was it. Benefiting from the drabness of the place as well as we could, and using it to really learn, we forced the daily number of prostrations up to 2,000 and from there to 3,000. Having to also eat, go to teachings, and keep contacts alive in Europe, that was our maximum. Then as now, letters were the big thing, the occupation of any unused moment. Also time was gained as we needed ever less sleep. Karmapa's blessing-field and the upwards-thrusting movement of the prostrations straightened out energy-channels to a point where we woke up rested after four to five hours. As the room was freezing, it was good to start early and work up a heat. To our amazement, the practice made our bodies into real gifts. They became tools to be used freely, and no hard work has been unpleasant since then.

Hannah's way of handling the prostrations impressed me deeply, the wisdom with which she handled such a taxing exercise. We did them side by side, she setting the rhythm, and as she is tough and keeps things flowing, there were no stops. We counted the ones she made while I did occasional quick bursts to provoke a stronger experience.

Combining the activity of body (the motion itself), of speech (the recitation used), and of mind (the meditation and awareness kept), prostrations are a total and transforming tantric practice. Lasting changes occur in people who do them, and there is no better way to

Hannah with nuns at Sonada

remove confused energy-streams from years of intoxicants, home-made philosophies, or inactivity than by putting one's system through this "horse cure." It is wise to trust the age-old wisdom of the practice as it is given, however. When I tried to improve on it, to shake my heart center loose by placing something hard where my chest hit the floor, there was little benefit. Though I did develop some interesting feelings around my heart, more lasting was a broken rib. My chest really hurt, and I had to do the last 30,000 supported only by my left arm, making more groans than mantras. Through the practice, lots of deep impressions matured. For a week, unaware what a fantastic blessing it was, the big black coat of the protector blocked out everything. It just hung there in front, unmoving.

The removal of so many drug-influences and wrong views frequently produced shakings and heavy grimacing. It was good to know that it was a purification, something dissipating and not something coming in. The last 10,000 flat-outs, belly-flops, or whatever else they were called, we did at 4,000 a day in the Bhutia Basty monastery in Darjeeling, with the ancient, charged-up Guru Rinpoche statue on our right. The lamas Thubten and Lody had made it possible, and Dr. Jigme and his family brought the food. On New Year's morning of

1971, the 111,111 prostrations were behind us, the first part of the foundation practices. We celebrated with a long, warm bath.

Returning to Sonada, Kalu Rinpoche gave an initiation. It was the first of countless empowerments we would receive from him. On this occasion, he transmitted the compassionate essence of all Buddhas, the white, four-armed Bodhisattva, now called Loving Eyes. In India during 1500 years, this force was known under the name of Avalokiteshvara, and the Tibetans translated it into Chenrezig. We squeezed ourselves right in front of Rinpoche's wonderfully carved face of so much timeless wisdom. His chanting and the sounds of his bell and drum were everywhere, and his face changed into ever new shapes. Suddenly I clearly saw the transparently white, four-armed Bodhisattva in front. The blessing was incredible, and afterwards my legs could hardly carry me. It was an initiation we never forgot.

Especially the Tibetans had a good laugh at my "improvement" of the prostrations. My rib felt the same in spite of bandages and exotic ointments put on by some very eager healers, however, and it was really out of style to be blocked by such a stupid obstacle. Also wishing to check out the Sunday market in Kalimpong, where genuine Tibetan artifacts were still surfacing, we decided to visit that interesting town at the first opportunity and also to try out the healing lama there.

Tashi from the Gompus Hotel had shared the ups and downs of our last visit. He knew quite well where we had been staying, which meant we were now inside the Tibetan system for gossip and information also there. What he didn't know, however, and was delighted to hear was our involvement with a traditional practice, that we planned to finish the four foundations. He guided us up the mountain to the Mongolian lama, buying newly-ground tsampa on the way, and it was a joy to feel how the ascent there, which we would formerly have experienced as cumbersome, was now pure pleasure. Through the prostrations our bodies had now found their beat and functioned flowingly and effortlessly. A very important step had been made. Our bodies were now good servants, not difficult masters. They no longer limited mind's freedom or made it lazy.

Arriving at the top of the ridge, we followed a wall of gray stones surrounding what was apparently a monastery. Then came a gate and a row of low huts inside. Tashi entered through the door at the far

At the entrance of Gompus Hotel

corner. Coming in from the glaring sun, the contrast was enormous. As our eyes got used to the darkness, however, a friendly-looking old man became visible. He sat at the end of a low room filled with boxes and bags, beckoning us to come in. We greeted him, and he gave his blessing in the way that Chechoo Rinpoche often does: placing both hands on the sides of one's head and then slowly moving them upwards towards the crown. At the same time, he invoked his protective Buddhas for us. We gave him the tsampa and some money as an offering. Then we told our story and he told his.

Like most Mongolians, he belonged to the school of the Gelugpas, literally the "Virtuous Ones." Though it is difficult to believe for a modern person, they actually chose that name themselves. Accordingly they are less known for spontaneous, yogic freshness than for organization and learning. They governed Tibet politically and founded monasteries, each housing thousands of monks, like the enormous Sera, Drepung, and Ganden. In these institutions, many monks passed exams in logic and the art of debate.

The ability to treat causes and not just effects is Buddha's great gift to the world; especially it targets the root cause of ignorance. Whether one prefers the way or total experience and meditation as in the three "old" or "Red Hat" schools or would rather study and learn as in this "reformed" or "Yellow Hat" one, for 1000 years Tibet has preserved Buddha's finest teachings. The quick way of devoted identification with Buddha and lama and the slow and steady one of gradual learning both are passed on and enable any talent, any development on any desired level.

This old Mongolian Lama—Tashi said he was about 100 years old, which he definitely didn't look—didn't fit the usual pattern. There was much more yogi than intellectual in him. His main practice was that of Choed, of "cutting off," an exciting meditation where one removes attachment at its root. Chanting a hauntingly beautiful tune with the musical support of a large hand drum, a bell, and a thighbone trumpet, in meditation one offers one's body to hungry ghosts and other needy beings while sending one's mind to one's lama. The practice is used in the old schools of Tibetan Buddhism, and the experiences during meditation can be most impressive. First, the invoked energies appear in the meditator's imagination, and then they really manifest. Whoever has mastered this total cutting-off of attachment can have a good laugh later at things which others fear and get upset about.

The Mongolian lama offered to teach us the practice right there and then, which was quite an honor. All we had to do was stay with him for six months in the local cemeteries. We wanted to finish the foundation practices first, however, with Kalu Rinpoche. Feeling the effectiveness of the first one in our bones, we could hardly wait to go on, and we knew enough to not just change meditations without first asking the guides for our present ones. That is a sure recipe for trouble. Therefore, after thanking him for his confidence and promising to take the teaching as soon as possible, we told him what we were already doing and under whom. Before leaving the lama, I remembered my rib, and he had a good laugh hearing how it had come about. Actually, the idea of placing something hard where my chest hit the floor came from a booklet by the Chinese yogi living down the hill, but he didn't seem to have heard of him. Tashi, however, knew him well. It was from his hotel that the infamous meat momos had been ordered!

The old lama took some gray-yellow powder out of two different bottles with a long spoon. Then he folded it into three square pieces of rice paper. With a chant of good wishes, he said, "These two you take with hot water tomorrow early and the day after, and this one with lukewarm water the evening between." The pain actually disappeared, and I've never felt that rib since, but whether the powders healed me or his direct influence, we are not sure . . . probably both working together.

Shortly after, it was time for Calcutta again. The police in Darjeeling couldn't extend our permits any longer, so now we had to visit their bosses for new ones. The young, well-educated man at the office in Writers' Building was no doubt put there by good karma and an influential father. He was sympathetic to us, and we to him. He promised to recommend us for a full six months in the Darjeeling area. As usual, we gave medical reasons for the stay, that Hannah needed the healthy air in the mountains to pick up strength after a bout of dysentery in Nepal. The officials probably suspected we were missionaries but had nothing against that. If we had ever said what our real reason for staying in the mountains was, they would have canceled any permit at once. They did this regularly to less experienced friends and would also try it on us some years later, though with little success. Tibetans to them are low caste and dirty, refugees who might be working undercover for the Chinese. It deeply disturbed them that Westerners, their secret idols, would now come to learn from the poorest refugees in their own country. Thus it soon became second nature for friends of Tibet to hide their beads and cover their blessing strings before going anywhere official.

While waiting for the permit, which was promised in ten days, we decided not to push it by returning to the mountains. Puri sounded better, a town on the Bay of Bengal. It lay south of Calcutta and was known as a pleasant winter site. Tourists and hippies both praised the place, and it was of a special interest to us because Joseph lived there. He was the former servant of W.Y. Evans-Wentz and had served him in the twenties in Sikkim. It meant he had been present while the professor obtained the first and probably best translations of some most important and formerly secret Tibetan texts. Shortly after the First World War, the masterly translations by the very learned Lama Kazi Dawa Samdub appeared in the four volume Oxford series as *The Tibetan Book of the Dead, The Tibetan Book of the Great Liberation, Tibet's Great Yogi Milarepa,* and *Tibetan Yoga and Secret Doctrines.*

Especially the last of these titles had been with us since jail. Here now was the chance to see someone who had been present at the very first meeting of two advanced cultures from which we hoped to make the best aspects merge. The northern European civilization which has spread around the world and Tibetan Buddhism simply complement each other on so many levels. Today, we still consider the direct translations in the four books first class, although most of the meditations cannot be practiced without much preparation and instruction. The commentaries, however, are confusing. Dr. Evans-Wentz did his doctorate on the druids of Celtic religion and simply could not fathom Buddhism. It benefits no one, and one loses all freshness and power by mixing the terminology and views of religious systems. Their ways and goals are just too different. It is much more useful for the world today to examine which religions benefit and free beings and to stop the ones which harm them.

Our meeting with Joseph did not quite reach the hoped for level of exchange; when his scared granddaughters dared open the door and let us in, Joseph was in bed and nearly unable to speak. We saw Evans-Wentz' top-hat and walking stick, but all the family talked about was their Hindu neighbors. They threw stones at them because they were Christian, and the granddaughters—otherwise quite attractive by the moustached local standard—could not find husbands.

In Puri we spent some fine days in a lodge near the beach, bathed in surprisingly unclear water, and ate mountains of food after so many prostrations. We learned the 100-syllable mantra by heart for the second part of the foundations, picked up on the latest events from the local hippies, and guided a group coming down from a bad aggressive trip. Some were also open to Buddhist wisdom and came to Sonada later. Every time I now spoke about Karmapa, something flowed through and the words just came by themselves. Actually it was good we did this extreme part of our development in a fool's paradise like India and not under the critical gaze of educated family and friends. It would have disturbed them that we hardly spoke any more of things which were not somehow connected to freeing the mind, that we saw any experience in only that light. Already then, the power of Buddha's teaching gathered mind's energy at a single awareness point. In addition to this, the repetition of mantra and mixing with Buddha-forms of energy and light was very effective. These methods dissolved ever faster whatever surfaced in the way of habits and disturbed feelings until there was only awareness. It was certain that development would now be automatic but also that this was only the beginning of a long journey.

CHAPTER FOURTEEN

Establishing a Practice

Returning to Sonada with the long-term permit, some fine news was waiting. A nearly forgotten application for Sikkim, filled out two months earlier, had been granted. It was right on time; Karmapa would now give the great Dolma Naljorma initiation at Rumtek. This important transmission, which each Karmapa gives only a few times, stretches over several days and is surrounded by other empowerments. Most of Kalu Rinpoche's Sonada group had already gone up. We hardly unpacked and went straight on, bringing along a hopeful Australian couple from Puri. Though they knew nothing of Karmapa and little about Buddhism, one day in the Western Himalayas they had applied for permits. Once again, all things connected with Karmapa fit perfectly. Today, the man has a high position helping the aborigines, and the woman supports a Theravada Centre near Sydney.

That same evening, we crossed the last bridge into Sikkim. Getting off the jeep at the Rumtek road eight kilometers before Gangtok, this time we wanted to walk the last stretch up. The weather was dry and crisp, and there is a quick footpath crossing the road again and again. On the last stretch it was already dark, and we kept bumping into cows and goats lying on the road. Most were still dragging the ropes and poles to which they had been tied. In the yard in front of the main building, a few naked bulbs supplied the light for a lot of people milling around. Hundreds of Tibetans and many high lamas had come from across the Himalayas for this event. There was only floor-space in the guest-house this time, and Yeshe, the local practical genius, spelled out the names of an impressive series of Rinpoches as the reason. The rooms were full to the brim, and we could imagine how many people he had to disappoint.

On the next morning, Karmapa started the preparatory ceremonies for the great initiation. We Westerners were in luck. Being both guests of the Tibetans and having arrived from the furthest distance are important factors in their culture. Accordingly, we were given seats directly in front, with an unobstructed view of Karmapa and his actions. One could physically feel what he was doing. Using a double hand drum, a bone-trumpet, and a bell, chanting and meditating without stop, he built up a power field around the hall. Gradually, the cows and goats we had stepped on the night before started walking the aisles. There was nothing for them to eat there, but apparently they were attracted by the goings-on. When major initiations were given, several of the valley's animals were known to tear themselves loose and find their way to the site. Their owners had already given up pulling them back as many just ran off again. Anyway, when it was over, most found their way back by themselves.

That night, all were tired but filled with blessing. Each had been given two stalks of kusha grass from Karmapa. During the night, the longer one should lie in the direction of one's body, while the shorter stalk should be under the pillow. While sleeping on this "T," all should watch their dreams. What came up this night might be of great significance.

I had two strong and clear dreams. In the first one, a Danish friend and I looked through a stack of very beautiful *thankas*. As I came to the scroll with the protector Black Coat, I pulled it to me, saying, "This one I want." With force it disappeared into my heart. In the second dream, I caught an old but stately Tibetan lady. She was falling down a slope, and I helped her up a mountain instead. I remembered a strong feeling of compassion and that the mountain gave a fantastic view. Hannah also had meaningful dreams, and in the morning we were both very pleased.

The initiation itself was even more impressive than the preparation. Dolma Naljorma is a protective Buddha aspect, a semi-wrathful green female form with eight arms. Under our disbelieving eyes, Karmapa actually began to look like her, taking on both her features

Tenga Rinpoche at the Black Hat Dances, Rumtek

Lama-dances at Rumtek, "Mahakala"

*Sangye Nyenpa Rinpoche
dancing in the yard
of Rumtek Monastery*

*Main Mahakala,
Big Black Coat,
Protector of the lineage,
Rumtek mask*

© Bianka Rohde

© Bianka Rohde

© Bianka Rohde

*Procession of Protectors at the Mahakala dances
streaming out of Rumtek Monastery*

and her youth. Only the color I didn't see, but there was no doubting the female energy flowing towards us. While he held the center of the power field, several incarnates walked through the rows of people. They touched everybody with charged-up objects carrying the power of his meditation, usually transferring their energy to our heads and hands. In such ways, the seeds of perfect enlightenment are planted and one is fully empowered. It is then possible to realize the essence of Buddha's body, speech, mind, qualities, and activity, to obtain his radiant unlimited nature. The power of Diamond Way initiations can bring beings to a state of liberation after death. When no sensory impressions confuse mind any more, beings with confidence in their potential may remove their illusion of a separate "I." Then, every event has the taste of liberation, of mind playing freely. From here, there is no falling back into lower forms of existence. As one level of insight gives way to the next, suddenly perceiver, perception, and object perceived stay one, and we have become Buddhas ourselves.

After physical death, no sense-impressions disturb mind. Then the wisdom forms one was initiated into arise from the store-consciousness as living fields of energy and light. Karmapa's Black Crown is very effective for this purpose. If one has kept one's bond to such expressions of timeless wisdom, one will enter their power field beyond time and space.

In "Great Way" Buddhism, the Pure Land of the red Buddha Limitless Light Amitabha, Opame, is invoked at death. As predominant desire is the cause of a human life, transforming this brings the quickest results. Whoever doesn't think that they will live forever are wise to repeat "OM AMI DEVA HRIH," the mantra of Limitless Light. Also one should take initiation into a Buddha of the Lotus family from a lama one trusts.

The initiation finished on the evening of the second day, and people returned to their quarters to digest it all. Hardly anybody talked, all were too full of the experiences of the day to even want to mention them. On the way back to the guest-house we met an impeccably clean-cut monk who must have been my age. As he knew some English and wanted contact with Westerners, during the following days we got to know him better. His name was Ayang Tulku, and he came from one of the smaller brother-lineages within the Kagyupa school.

Although the three old or "Red Hat" schools of Tibetan Bud-dhism have methods for transferring beings' consciousness at death, this lineage often taught it to large groups of people collectively, also checking their results. This meditation enables the awareness-force of one's mind to consciously leave the body. Going out from a place on the top of one's head, about eight fingers back from the original hairline, it fuses with the awareness of the red Buddha Limitless Light. The outer sign of success is a small wound, a pimple, a drop of blood, or lymph at the place where mind's energy broke the skin. The inner experience when dying is much stronger than during practice but also involves moving upwards through a tube of light. Then one flies from one's body and enters a state of bliss and awareness, which is totally beyond anything known. This joyful, perfect experience will con-stantly increase in meaning and dimensions until every limiting concept dissolves. It is the power field of Limitless Light, his so-called "Pure Land," and teaching this practice to 26000 students around the world from 1987 to 1997 has been an immense joy. I now give Phowa courses about twelve times a year.

Ayang Tulku's dream had also been auspicious. He had met Kunzig Shamarpa, the emanation of Limitless Light, asked his bless-ing, and offered him fruit. He added some information on Tibetan ways of interpreting dreams. Afterwards, he talked about the Tibetan camps between Bangalore and Mangalore where he lived. It was new to us that thousands of Tibetans from the high plateau beyond the Himalayas were now living in the tropical climate of southern India which is so unhealthy for them. Most of these groups were nomads from western Tibet, and they had fled seven years after everyone else. Leaving animals, tents, and most belongings behind, they had come to India in 1966 during the Chinese Cultural Revolution. The Communist Chinese, who claimed that these very docile refugees were criminals, pressured India to send them back. For this reason, they were transported from the northern border to a formerly unin-habited jungle in the south. Maybe a third of them died; the shock of change was simply too much, but the survivors had rich opportunities to show their natural skills. With amazing speed, they managed the sudden jump from arctic nomads to farmers in a jungle and were already showing the local Indians that diligence would make the soil yield good crops. Ayang Tulku was keenly interested in having us visit and help him there, and we promised to keep the contact and not forget the things he had asked us for.

During the next days, Karmapa gave a series of other initiations. Quite a strange Canadian lama had also appeared, who held his students on a very short leash. It was the first Western teacher we had seen, and Hannah and I found him theatrical. Karmapa, however, did not expose him. Planting the joy, wisdom, compassion, activity, and protective power of all Buddhas in those present, he activated a series of energies that may all bring about Buddhahood. Until the ending of the foundation practices, such initiations are rather a blessing than the beginning of a practice, but we knew they would give depth also to the meditations lying directly ahead. Apparently Karmapa had pulled some official strings this time, and all could stay for the ten days that were needed. We were thankful not to have to confront the Indians for that.

Back at Sonada, it was now time for the 111,111 repetitions of the hundred syllable mantra of Diamond Mind (Vajrasattva, Dorje Sempa) and the meditation going with it. As one has to articulate each syllable, to somebody in good shape this stage often takes longer than the prostrations. Diamond Mind is the purifying power of all Buddhas, and the practice has immense force. As harmful impressions leave one's store-consciousness, mind enjoys itself ever more and finally relaxes enough to recognize its luminous perfect nature.

Nothing in the conditioned world can even get close to mind's perfect state. The mere fact of not being enlightened is basically flawed. And how? Buddha explains this painful, pervading phenomenon in the following way: out of timeless ignorance, which is in mind like clouds are in the sky, the illusion of duality appears, a separation between subject, object, and action. Thus mind attaches itself to its emptiness-nature, its "space," thinking "I," and experiences its clarity-nature, whatever is happening in that space, as a "you" or something "other." From this feeling of separation, the basic disturbing states appear: attachment to what one likes and aversion against what one doesn't like. Attachment leads to greed, as one naturally wants to keep what is pleasant, and aversion becomes envy. Few wish their enemies to do well. Finally ignorance produces the stupid, exclusive pride. This appears from the illusion that one's present transient state is something real, that it could somehow be better than those of others, who also have no true solidity or essence.

Buddha furthermore teaches that there are 84,000 possible combinations of these disturbing feelings and that all negative actions, words, and thoughts appear from them. They lead to harmful habits and produce the veils, which keep mind from experiencing its enlightened nature. Though these hindrances are felt to be so very real when present, they never had more substance than the dust on a mirror. Therefore both beings' illusions and the suffering arising from them can be removed. To bring this about, all Buddhas united their purifying power in the form of Diamond Mind. His radiantly clear, kind, and indestructible awareness is able to clean out and dissolve the countless subconscious knots in anybody's mind. Life being as it is, even if not engaged in the above practices, a few repetitions of the 100-syllable mantra before sleep is one of the most intelligent habits one can develop. It clears the slate for the next day.

The process of purification is most effective after having understood the dynamics of cause and effect, karma, and how unwished-for results maybe deflected. Here follows the essence of the many teachings we have had from our lamas on this subject, and whoever wants to know more may refer to my book, *The Way Things Are*, also with Blue Dolphin Publishing. All of causality—its arising, its effects, and its dissolution—can be seen as three groups of four conditions. Here is a short summary:

For impressions, "Karma," to be planted in beings' minds that will cause later happiness or suffering, one or several of four conditions must be met.

1. One must be aware how a situation is.
2. One must wish for something to happen.
3. One must do it oneself or have others do it.
4. One must be satisfied afterwards.

More conditions working together and factors which increase their intensity also strengthen their effect. Likewise, the results manifest in four ways:

1. In one's experience after death, when mind's content of subconscious impressions matures. This happens due to the lack of new sensory input, and the projections produced are experienced as

being real. They bring joy or fear, greed or confusion, jealousy or attachment. Within not more than seven weeks, the strongest set of impressions solidifies into one of the six states of existence.

When again, maybe after a very long time, mind unites with a human body, three further results follow.

2. The kind of body to which a mind is attracted. This means the kind of genes that fit it. This causes health and a long life or the opposite.

3. The surroundings into which one is born—whether it is among the 10% in rich or 90% in poor countries, in the suburbs or ghettos of the world. Sexual harm inflicted upon others, for instance, brings rebirth in desert-conditions; whereas very good karma, mixed with wrong views, produces conditions like in northwestern Europe.

4. And finally, one's habitual tendencies that will produce new karma. Whether, for instance, one is naturally friendly and warm to others or controlling and unpleasant.

After this overview of the patterns of cause and effect that bind all unenlightened beings, now, how to break this messy and beginningless chain?

Also through four steps:

1. One reaches the conviction that something in life is not satisfactory, that one is still not enlightened, experiences painful states of mind, has harmed or cannot do enough for others, or whatever.

2. One purifies mind, using for quickest results effective Diamond Way methods, like the meditations on Diamond Mind.

3. One promises not to repeat harmful actions or words, taking this promise again whenever broken.

4. Consciously one tries to do only positive things. There is much joy and relief in nullifying whatever suffering one has formerly caused.

"No act exists, no matter how serious, which will not be purified through these four steps," Kalu Rinpoche often said. "However, they only help if you use them. What benefit is a bar of soap," he continued, "if you just keep it in your pocket? Even in a hundred years it won't make you clean. Only practice brings results."

In no way disturbed that Rinpoche prescribed the same medicine for everyone, we started the 111,111 hundred-syllable purification mantras. Above our heads, as best we could, we held the crystal form of Diamond Mind, wishing that he would free our store-conscious-ness of whatever impressions blocked it. After the first few repetitions of the mantra, we already felt the power field of Diamond Mind condensing and then flowing down through us. Although all kinds of disturbing feelings—especially irritations—came up during the sessions, we understood them to be a zoological garden leaving our minds. It was good to know that they were just the tip of an iceberg of obstacles. Many difficulties would have manifested later if not broken down now through the practice. Meditating on our bed in the Crees house with frequent strands of clouds passing through the open windows, we easily spent up to sixteen hours a day. Though it was a relief to burn the seeds of future troubles, it took long to make our knees used to sitting after the many prostrations.

The purification-mantras convincingly removed the results of former negative actions. Countless—but fair—fist-fights and many drug-induced blocks in the inner channels dissolved in the constant flow of nectar, and gradually robot-like reactions changed. They became more flowing and fit a wider variety of situations. Towards the end of the practice came strong dreams. They were right out of the text-book—wrestling black giants, drinking milk, and throwing up ink—and showed the process to be a success. We felt as though we were walking on air.

CHAPTER FIFTEEN

Bodhisattvahood

At this time, we heard that a visa for Sikkim had again arrived. By now we automatically reapplied on the day of return. Thus another visit would coincide with important outer events. The fact that we were the only foreigners at Rumtek at the time made the impression especially lasting.

Sitting in front of Karmapa, we were just answering his questions about the advanced meditations we had done earlier from various books. We described how we had felt immense blessing and power without even knowing that such things as Refuge and Initiation existed. While he explained that in spite of such strong experiences they could bring no lasting effects without his blessing, that the Foundations were actually more effective at this stage, something happened that at first we didn't understand.

In a side remark, Karmapa had just asked me the time, that I should tell him without looking at my watch. I was about a quarter of an hour off, and he said one would always be completely accurate when the inner channels were totally purified. With this still on his lips, suddenly his eyes rolled back as we had seen quite a few times. Without a word, he rose and went into the next room. We heard his recitation, his bell, and hand drum and were certain that he was now calling in and transferring the mind of someone who had died, bringing it to a pure level of experience. "Who went?" we asked ourselves, and the monks running everywhere looked just as surprised. Two hours later, while Karmapa was still alone in the room, the radio gave the answer. It spread like fire. The King of Bhutan, a great sponsor of Rumtek and a disciple of Karmapa, had just died in Nairobi of a heart attack. Karmapa had apparently already transferred his consciousness.

The Bhutanese king, like the very competent one governing today, had been educated in England. Forgetting the power of his roots, he had adopted the educated, materialistic views of his time. When he came back to take over his country, however, Karmapa was in Bhutan. He reminded the King of mind's potential in a traditional way. By stating the bodily signs, family-conditions, birth times, and other details of three incarnations who had been sought by their monasteries for several years, now these important positions could be filled. The boys lived in some remote Bhutanese valleys. The King immediately had them picked up and all information was accurate, although Karmapa had never been in that part of the country himself. In addition, the children were tested in the traditional way, choosing among similar objects the ones they had used in their former life. They also recognized several old attendants. Deeply impressed that such powers exist, the King became Karmapa's disciple. It was a wise choice. After enjoying a rich and meaningful life, it had now brought him liberation after death. A very important activity survived him. The King had become a great sponsor of Buddhism. He had used his influence and material means freely to support the three "old" schools of Tibetan Buddhism that so rarely get anything from official sources. In the supposedly spiritual East, this function is just as important as in the West today. Without a church or supportive community to pick up the bills, nothing happens. One must use the means of the conditioned world to get out of it, and a lack of generosity is a frequent bottleneck for our work everywhere. Those who choose Buddhism because idealists ask no fixed fees get very cheap blessing indeed!

Already on the next day, Karmapa took fifty lamas along to Bhutan. He was needed for the burial ceremony and the enthrone-ment of the new king. His head was completely shaved, and as usual when building up special energies, his body seemed larger and his voice was very loud. As he crossed the yard on his way to the jeep, the protective energies around him were a near-visible field of power. A fold of his robe touched me while walking past, and it felt like an electric shock.

Before leaving, Karmapa told us to stay in Rumtek with the four young incarnates: Kunzig Shamarpa and the Situ, Gyaltsap, and Jamgon Kongtrul Rinpoches. He wanted us to take the Bodhisattva vows with Shamar Rinpoche, their senior.

This was the opportunity to get to know them better and for them to ask innumerable questions about the West. The Indians actually seemed to have forgotten us for the moment. For once in Rumtek, there were no excited calls. Shamar Rinpoche explained the Bodhisattva-vow, and the others sat around. Adding their budding English to our few Tibetan and Nepali words, we managed to clarify the main points. Mixing minds with them in the vast hall, while surrounded by hundreds of reciting monks, was a lasting experience. Returning in the jeep, we felt them sitting in our hearts and continuing the explanation. It was an amazing ride!

While the outer vows help beings avoid trouble and also free their energies for spiritual development, the secret or "tantric" vows taken during initiations or mind-teachings like the Great Seal transform our ordinary world into a pure Buddha field. The Bodhisattva vow bridges these two levels and confers the power to work altruistically. The effect of each positive action is increased immeasurably when done for the good of everybody, and also one's view on suffering is profoundly altered. Unpleasant events now shift from being painful purifications to becoming a part of one's schooling. Experiencing them consciously provides the wisdom to help others in similar situations later.

The Bodhisattva vow consists of two parts. The first is about motivation. One decides to become enlightened for the good of all beings, to avoid anger, and not exclude anybody from one's good wishes. This in no way means turning the other cheek. Putting up with harmful behavior just means giving certain people and cultures more rope to hang themselves. Instead one should work unsentimentally with the causes of pain, not the effects. Today that would mean helping poor countries and levels of society to have many fewer children and to educate the ones they get. Compassion in the form of intelligent, far-reaching actions bring real results. It effectively removes the causes for most aggression, and later no suffering will

Kunzig Shamar Rinpoche

Tai Situpa

Kongtrul Rinpoche

Gyaltsap Rinpoche

surface. Skillfully removing any cause of anger is vitally important because nothing destroys good karma as thoroughly as this very feeling. If one falls from the highest motivation of emptiness and compassion, however, if one begins to experience what happens as real and reacts negatively, all isn't lost. One can still purify the anger and should do that as soon as possible. Thus its destructive power is defused, and with relief one will soon notice how envy and hatred gradually diminish.

The second part of the vow concerns practical life. Here one decides on the deeds, words, and thoughts that benefit beings and may bring them to enlightenment. They are called the six liberating actions. They are:

1. **Generosity.** Including body, speech, and mind, material things, education, and protection. Generosity makes a fine bridge to other beings and fills mind with richness. It means not keeping pleasant things and experiences to oneself, but to instead share freely, seeing giver, receiver, and gift as parts of the same totality.

2. **Right livelihood.** One cannot use the word "morality" here because that has always been used by church and state to control people. For a thousand years, if the state didn't catch them during life, the church would put them in hell afterwards. The term means using body, speech, and mind skillfully, doing what brings long-time happiness, and avoiding the causes of harm.

3. **Patience.** It mainly means to avoid anger. In this way, one can avoid destroying the good impressions collected through the former two actions.

4. **Diligence, or joyful energy.** It helps one constantly enlarge given possibilities, to never be satisfied with the obtained results, but to keep developing. Lovers, lawyers, artists, all recognize the usefulness of these four actions. They are generally considered fine qualities also by those who don't understand about enlightenment.

In this system, **meditation (5)** does not mean highest methods for realizing the nature of mind. Rather its goal is to create distance. With that, one can consciously choose the comedies of life and avoid its tragedies. Gradually, theoretical insight becomes a full experience and benefits also one's practical situation. Such meditation of "calming and holding" mind (Shine, Shamatha) is the foundation for later and really exciting methods.

H.H. Shamarpa,
1985

6. Liberating Wisdom. This is not yet spontaneous insight but still has concepts. If the first five are seen as strong legs bringing one forward, this insight is like the clear eyes showing one where to go. Its essence is knowing that doing good is natural because subject, object, and action are all interdependent, and what one gives out, one gets back.

These six are a great beginning, and when they have been perfected, another four become possible, which are rarely mentioned. In Tibetan the terms are *Thab, Monlam, Thob,* and *Yeshe,* and they translate as special methods, strong good wishes, strength, and ultimate wisdom. Being self-arisen, non-dual, and immediate, this state makes one faultless in benefiting all beings.

During a touching ceremony with much deep-voiced chanting, Kunzig Shamarpa gave us the Bodhisattva vow. We both wiped our eyes a lot while it went on. In the beginning the vow was not easy to keep. The first test came shortly after, when the Indians asked us to leave Sikkim once more. Over a long period, we sometimes had to completely freeze our thoughts. Gradually, however, the vow proved a blessing without end. It even made the aggressive people whom I used to "dust off" take their trip elsewhere. The "outer" vows of not killing, stealing, lying, etc., one only takes once, that is, as long as one hasn't broken them and hopes to restore them. The "inner" or Bodhisattva vow, however, one may strengthen with teachers whom one considers to be such. Also one should remember it daily in one's mind. There is surely no finer motivation for a life than the wish to benefit all beings.

CHAPTER SIXTEEN

First Return

BACK AT SONADA, we began the mandala offerings. They are the third part of the foundation meditations and a sheer pleasure. During this practice, which is also repeated 111,111 times, one places seven small heaps of colored rice on a metal plate. Imagining them to be everything precious in the universe, one keeps a simplified representation of the Refuge in front and presents everything without attachment. Then one wipes the heaps of rice into a cloth and builds up another perfect world, which is once more offered up. Also in this practice, body, speech, and mind work together. Thus the result is nothing conceptual but rather an enrichment of one's totality. After a hundred of these short offerings, at that time in Sonada one made a longer one of the 37 desirable objects of a traditional Asian universe. They include elephants, dancing-girls, and skillful generals winning one's wars. Having basked in traditional pleasures, one can then return to BMW motorcycles, sports-cars, Rolo trendy clothing, Blue Green Algae, modern girls, or disco nights—to all that may bring sparkle to people's lives today.

The mandala offerings are the shortest of the practices; one can finish them in about twenty days. Also here we made the last ten thousand in front of the great Guru Rinpoche statue in the Bhutia Basty monastery. This building has a history that we sometimes told when American missionaries cornered us on buses and would not leave us alone. We always tried to avoid this embarrassing waste of time by saying that religion should be seen as medicine, that their only function is to help beings. Therefore, those interested should examine

The Bhutia Basty monastery which was moved down from the Mahakala Hill

what might best suit them and let others find their thing. As long as religions don't make their followers suppress women or make "holy" wars, they were nobody else's business. The less educated among the missionaries were very insistent, however, and kept pushing until one scared them by transcending their horizon or stepped seriously on their toes. It then always brought nice long pauses in the conversation to tell the following story about forcing others in spiritual matters.

The Bhutia Basty monastery, dedicated to the Buddhist Protectors, was earlier situated on the high point of the hill on the side of which it now stands. It is the triangular wood-covered peak behind the Chow Rastra square and the Windermere Hotel in Darjeeling, with the beggars along the path. It had been built there because the protector Mahakala had manifested on this site several times. Around the turn of the century, the English had the monastery pulled down and rebuilt at the place where it now stands. They wanted a church on the excellent location instead, which offers a view of Nepal, Sikkim, and Bhutan. Hardly had they finished the building, however, when it collapsed for no apparent reason. They rebuilt it; again it fell down, and the process repeated itself a third time. Today there is a Mahakala place on this hill again, but its left side has been taken over by Hindus and local religions. The English built their church on the main street of Darjeeling instead, and today it is a cinema. Nobody had any benefit at all.

Karmapa stayed long in Bhutan. After the King's death, much had to be done, and he found new incarnations and gave initiations across the country. When we had just finished the mandala offerings, Kalu Rinpoche and his nephew Gyaltsen also drove there, leaving us very thankful. They had just used our rice from the mandala offerings during some great ceremonies in their temple.

Shortly before leaving, he pulled one of those tricks which teachers may play on people for their own good. Some alcoholic Sherpas regularly came to the monastery, not to contribute but to complain. This time their subject was the weather: The rains were a month late and their harvest might suffer. Kalu Rinpoche knew them well. They were also weekend Communists and walked in drunk and noisy demonstrations through town. When seeing him in the street, they left the procession, ran over for a quick blessing, and then resumed shouting in all directions. Bokhar Tulku was an especially sensitive Rinpoche of some northern Tibetan nomadic tribes, who was brought up by Kalu Rinpoche and spent most of his time in retreat. He always turned pale when he was invited by the wild Sherpas to make pujas. Kalu Rinpoche did nothing to protect him, however. With a wry smile he sent him again and again to their drunken festivities.

In the Darjeeling area, only a few valleys from their homeland, the Sherpas had fallen victim to cheap political slogans. Somehow the balanced people we had met in Nepal had here become sour and frustrated. Without the backing of an own Buddhist culture, the relationship between religion and alcohol had become disturbed, and they slanted heavily towards the easier of the two. Now they had come again to ask for rain, "You shall get what you need," Rinpoche said and looked unusually angelic, as he often did when teaching somebody a lesson. Accordingly, we kept our eyes open for what would come. And it did! Within a few hours, black clouds moved up the hill, and the water came down in buckets. Everything was flooded, and in many places the edges of the terraced fields were washed down. People had to work in the streaming rain to repair the damage, while we tried to remember what so much water felt like with a hangover.

Karmapa always built people up. He made everybody feel the greatest, until stupid habits and former karmas pulled them off their high horses again. Again he built them up, and this process went on until both ups and downs became exciting manifestations of mind's potential. Any moment we forgot the personal stuff and focused on bringing others to lasting enlightenment, we were automatically his partners, not students. Kalu Rinpoche, on the other hand, worked on a much more personal level. He went out of his way to take a punch at people when he saw them getting too smug. He then provoked situations where they would very quickly observe how far their work with the mind had progressed. When for instance his group built up a "good" bourgeois Buddhist morality, a horror to Hannah and me but which Rinpoche's less exciting students easily got into, he was aware at once. The same happened when they developed stiff ideas about subjects which they didn't yet know from their own experience. Hardly changing his tone of voice, Rinpoche then quickly turned from his orthodox teaching to stories about "holy freaks," such as Drugpa Kunle.

Drugpa Kunle was a Bhutanese yogi and devotee of Karmapa. He had an awakened compassion for the fair sex and developed thousands in close situations. Excerpts from his life story have now appeared in English, and though his teaching style calls for more power and presence than most can invest, he is a recognized example of enlightened activity. Every action of his led beings towards liberation or shook people out of their conditioned thoughts and ideas. What everyone can learn from, whether they practice avoidance, motivation, or pure view, are his words spoken loudly to the Buddha in Jokhang, the main temple of Lhasa: "There you are, enlightened because you thought of others, and here am I, who only thought of myself."

Kalu Rinpoche also knew how to get to Hannah and me. We, especially I, always feel excellent. Events we don't find nice we at least find interesting. There is always enough space around difficult situations and the inclination to turn them into a joke. Hannah is so harmonious that she is usually only hurt by the suffering of others, whereas my mind finds all experience exciting. Only in one field were we open to attack: in the area of our love, of our attachment to one another. It runs in our families. Our parents and also their parents were very close. They were the two-headed beings, the functioning couples where the man becomes the woman's power and joy and the woman his intuitive wisdom and openness. We felt a complete unity, and every separation was unpleasant. Kalu Rinpoche, of course, knew this, so in April when we happily came to ask his blessing for our third wedding anniversary, he smiled and said, "How nice. Now for the next three years you can become monk and nun. That will be good for you." If his goal was making us angry, he succeeded. During the next hours we had to consciously freeze our minds to avoid thoughts that we would have to purify afterwards.

For the fourth and last part of the foundation practices, Guru Yoga, we needed further teachings. It consists of a long introductory stage where one opens up to the lineage. Then follow some high mind teachings, several wishes for enlightenment, and finally comes a repetition that calls in the blessing of all Buddhas. As Kalu Rinpoche was still gone and we would take these teachings from no one else, there was now a waiting period. As usual it all fit, however, and no time was lost. During these days, several future contacts showed up in Sonada. Kim Wuensch, Nick and Eva, Ole and Hanne, Klaus and Rikke and Hara were some whose karma had ripened at this time and who came for Karmapa's blessing. It now made excellent sense that Kalu Rinpoche had asked us to pass his teachings on, and it was an additional joy to share the local Buddhist sites for which we never had time. When Rinpoche and Gyaltsen returned, all of Sonada received him on the tracks of the baby railroad. In the meantime, Hannah and I had also discovered how much we liked this old warrior. After his blessing, the feeling of his hands stayed on my head for a long time.

In the Crees house, we Westerners had been living in Nepali style for too long. We were simply too many in too few rooms, and there was too much meaningless talk. It was a relief that our friends could now start formal practices, and we could continue our own. After a shared initiation into Loving Eyes, Kalu Rinpoche made me explain the inner meditation for the first time, and thus they were on their way. It was an honor. To teach the Diamond Way, one has to be sure of all details and be an acceptable example to others at the same time. If people lose trust because one displays strange behavior, even the finest method is useless.

With instructions on the last foundation practice, Hannah and I could finally begin. Our motivation had actually been strengthened during the interim. Surrounded by old friends, our newly-found sensitivities had been repelled by the habits, thoughts, and expressions that surfaced. It was evident that we needed additional distance not to get caught by them again, and there was also no doubt that this was necessary. With a shudder, we realized that their roots were to a great extent exactly those feelings that Kalu Rinpoche had exposed as mental poisons: attachment, anger, greed, and pride. Such insights made us all the happier to again have time for our minds.

While we neared the end of the foundations, the atmosphere around Sonada changed. One saw more suffering than before, as the war in eastern Pakistan brought many refugees into the mountains. From our house it was only ten kilometers to the front, and I was sometimes sure we heard cannon fire in the distance, although it was difficult to distinguish it from the frequent thunder of the monsoon. On every trip to Darjeeling, the roads were full of East Pakistani refugees in their pink cotton robes. They were freezing in the alien climate and had deeply red, infected eyes. Also on a trip to Calcutta they were highly visible. Each of the cement segments originally intended for a water supply and left unused along the railway for years was now the "home" of an entire refugee family.

Some practical people from the group had volunteered to help, which was definitely not wanted, and what happened to the aid sent by the West was more than doubtful. We did our repetitions with an ominous feeling of things breaking up. There were several signs that the retreat in Sonada was finishing and that a period of traditional learning had come to an end. Becoming steadily more aware of how difficult it is to obtain harmonious outer conditions for an undisturbed practice, we spurred ourselves on to use every moment left.

The foreign police had already informed us that they wanted a chat. The officials in Delhi had discovered that we were using our applications for a student visa to stay in the restricted areas. We were in no way studying in the lowlands at a Hindu university as they

would have liked. Now we had the charming choice of either leaving
the mountains or leaving the country. We composed a friendly,
meaningless letter, which, with the speed of the bureaucracy there,
should have provided us with a few more months of "free air," but in
this case it didn't work. Although several of the officials in Darjeeling
were Buddhists and therefore delayed the whole thing for us, some big
boys further up the ladder in Delhi had become sharp, and shortly
thereafter we were again presented with the same two possibilities.
This time we sent them a doctor's medical report but knew that they
would not accept this for long either. In the middle of this race to
finish the practices in Sonada, something struck us like lightning. A
neurotic American fleeing the Vietnam War ran into our room and
yelled, "Kalu Rinpoche is leaving for America. They are packing
already." This was in the autumn of 1971, and though we considered
ourselves cool and ready for anything, the news was such a shock that
I had to run straight to the toilet. Could that be true? We were in a
fever.

It was. The time had come to bring the activity of all Buddhas to
the West, and many traditional teachings of Milarepa and the
Karmapa's would be given by this old lama. He, Gyaltsen, and the
nun Ani Chogar had just heard from Karmapa that their (Bhutanese)
passports were ready.

Among the events during these last days of turmoil, one clearly
showed how Buddhism can reach animals. A large, yellow dog came
under the wheels of a jeep in Darjeeling and was run over in the
middle. We jumped there at once, and repeating "OM AMI DEVA
HRIH," I put my meditation beads on top of its head. It showed
absolutely no signs of panic, and as a gush of blood came from its
mouth and it died, we knew that it was going to something better. On
top of the joy that it worked, we were also very thankful.

As a farewell gift to his students, shortly before leaving, Kalu
Rinpoche gave an initiation of "Long Life." This time many Tibetans
came, and he blessed all with his charged-up objects. He removed
obstacles to beings' lives, increasing instead the qualities which
prolong them. During the process, to my amazement, a place in my
right hand became hot and painful. As I looked, a new and deep
furrow was appearing in my palm, which is otherwise marked by few

H.H. Karmapa and the highest lineage-holders
blessing a stupa built by Kalu Rinpoche at Sonada

but clear lines. Very impressed, but without knowing what it meant, we took it as a tune-up: the Buddhas were also preparing us to bring the teachings West.

It was touching to see the Tibetans take leave of Kalu Rinpoche. They cling so much to their teachers that every departure is a real amputation. It is a main point in the teaching not to see the Lama as a person but rather as a mirror showing one's own perfection, as an expression of everybody's Buddha-mind. However, most still attach themselves to the outer physical form. It may add to the blessing felt but will also make one vulnerable. While our Tibetan friends were suffering, we Westerners were in high gear. So now it would happen! Kalu Rinpoche was going to the West, and our friends would be able to see him. Fantastic!

Several of Rinpoche's Western students traveled with him from Sonada. Sherab Tharchin paid for the party's voyage on his expense account. Two Canadians, Ken and Ingrid, also came along. They had just finished the foundations. Dennis and Rosemary, a French couple, went ahead to organize in Paris.

On his way to America, Kalu Rinpoche visited Israel, the Pope in Rome, and then Paris. Here he stayed for three weeks, and several of our friends went to see him. My brother, Bjorn, got our letter on his farm in Sweden, filled a Volvo with friends, and drove a thousand miles straight down. Just as he thought that maybe it was time to start looking for the address, they were in front of the house. Racing up the stairs, they landed right in an initiation into Loving Eyes. From Paris, Kalu Rinpoche flew to North America, where he was stuck for a year. Having given Sherab Tharchin, his sponsor, unsolicited sexual advice, the latter became annoyed and would not pay for his return.

Also for us, the months in Sonada were over. The messages from Delhi became ever more threatening, and it wasn't fair to let the police cover our stay any longer. However, we had learned to milk the various offices, which seemed to have no idea what the others were doing. Therefore, we once again went down the hill to Siliguri and obtained two extra weeks. This was exactly what was needed to finish the last practice. At the end of this period, a visa for Sikkim came from yet another office, and joyfully we went up to Karmapa.

It was wonderful to be with friends in Rumtek again. The place had really become our "pure land." Again Karmapa gave a series of initiations, among them "Highest Bliss" (Chakra Samvara, Pal Khorlo Demchok) and others of the most practiced in our lineage. The Tibetans were amazed at my grimacing, which was still brought about by the strong influx of energy. They saw it as an expression of strong devotion, but above all it meant that my upper inner channels still needed some work. However, the shaking of my body was nearly gone. Between the initiations Gelongma Palmo, the stately English nun, gave some teachings on our next practice. It was the meditation on the eighth Karmapa and his energy-field. As her Tibetan was not good and she did embody a strong Christian, Hindu, and Gelugpa background, some of her instructions we had to discard later.

Once again the Indian officials freaked out, especially the notorious Mr. Das in Gangtok. He took it personally that we always overstayed in the country and felt that this time we had really gone too far. We had sent out an application for an extension with somebody who had to go via Calcutta first. We telephoned him, but of course he wouldn't prolong anything and even threatened to send soldiers if we didn't leave the country at once. I was super-friendly on the phone, really enjoyed showing that he couldn't make us angry anymore, but also this new approach gave no extra time. So with Karmapa's help we had to very quickly decide where now to go. Ourselves we thought of Nepal and our friendly Lama Chechoo, but Karmapa had other plans for us: "You go home," he said. "Home? Where home?" we asked. "Home to Europe, of course," Karmapa said.

That was a deep punch. Every other possibility had been in our minds. If not Nepal, then maybe Ceylon or, with Karmapa's blessing, possibly even Bhutan. But Europe? We could not imagine anything more foreign than that. Karmapa's words were like a dip in ice water, however. After getting over the first shock, the idea was invigorating. We were ready, and being allowed to stand on our own legs now was the greatest of challenges. Holding and developing what we had learned as the first Western group and in so alien a culture would be a good sized job.

As we took our leave, Karmapa gave us a beautiful *thanka*. It depicted the Buddha-aspects expressing the compassion, wisdom, and power of mind. He promised to keep his blessing with us and had a truck drive us to the Gangtok road, where a jeep was already waiting. Suddenly we were on our way back to Europe with his last words in our ears, "We are always together." We took the detour via Darjeeling to let the police clear themselves by officially throwing us out and from there the train to Delhi. After one or two days in the house of a quaint lady who would only board Scandinavians, a telegram came with a hundred dollars from our parents. With the fifty we still had, it should have been enough for the trip, which at that time cost about seventy-five dollars. We quickly found Jacques, a big strong Frenchman. He was taking his old Beford bus back to Europe. Although the prices had suddenly jumped to a hundred dollars for each, he still took Hannah and me for what we had, even throwing in a daily meal. As he could easily have filled his bus at the full price, he was really kind.

So in this style we left India. We meditated at the front window and kept Jacques awake, while with great skill and constant honking he drove his flock of fifty hippies through the masses of people, animals, cars, and carriages in India and Pakistan. The cold nights in

Afghanistan really hurt. After two years, our cheap sleeping bags were now as thin as paper, and we fully understood the former sun worshippers of the area. One especially evil night, with all our extra clothes piled over Hannah and me up every half hour to jump around, we were in luck. Just as it was becoming really unpleasant, some enormous, clean-smelling, and apparently vermin-free dogs appeared from the desert with heads as big as ours. Short-haired and cream-colored, they lay down on both sides of us and kept our Asia-weakened bodies warm. In return, they received blessings and man-tras until dawn made it possible to move on. Jacques drove tirelessly, with only a few hours of sleep at night but lots of meals instead. Though the steering of the bus was nearly nonexistent, as I discovered when taking turns with him, every day brought us closer to Europe.

In Istanbul we stopped for a day or two, changing passengers and visiting familiar places. They were much less charming now without smoke in our lungs. Worst was the Gulhane Hotel, for years the central meeting-place for the drug scene between Europe and Asia. The place was no joke. One could have declared the building a hospital and started treatment at once. Everybody there was more or less sick, and the worst cases of hepatitis were luminous in a deep golden-green. Also, the mental atmosphere had changed. The shared openness and idealistic comradeship of two years earlier had disap-peared. The Turks now threw people in jail for thirty years just for having hash, and for a Westerner to survive even a few years there was hardly possible. So everyone was paranoid. Recently, an American had been caught. Knowing that his government would not help him, he had snatched a machine gun from a policeman and cleaned out the station before being shot.

Turkey, as well as anything Moslem, was of course Asia. Bulgaria and Yugoslavia were indefinable. In Graz, beautiful, cultural, free, and many-faceted Europe came on with full power. Here we knew that we had arrived. Already in 1971, and for the first time anywhere, I consciously decided to start a Buddhist center in this town. It must have been a lucky wish! In Graz today, some of my closest students guide two excellent Centers, a smaller one in town and a large one outside town. With joy, we again experienced European houses, saw how clean and big they are and with such precise angles. Though still crawling along in our old bus towards Holland, it was a great and free feeling to see people travel at above 100 miles per hour along the Autobahn. It struck us that here the taxis drove faster in reverse than most cars in India do in their forward gears. It was wonderful to feel the limitless possibilities of a place with so much raw, fresh energy. Europe came on beautifully after so long in a slow part of the world.

We met my loving parents, who had driven down to Amsterdam. With tears of joy, we fell into each other's arms and had a fine trip home to Denmark in their car. Also Hannah's parents were wonderful, and within days, much of our gang appeared. Quickly, the word spread that this Diamond Way must be something really effective, humanizing such a troublemaker as their old friend Ole so thoroughly. Although we rarely noticed it ourselves, seeing everything in the light of our new "thing," we were markedly different from the people who had left Copenhagen two years earlier.

Our first job, we decided, was to make available to others what we had learned ourselves. It was important to teach the Diamond Way in a form that could bridge cultural differences to the West. Many good people were badly confused by exotic and misleading books and would benefit from a clear presentation of Tibetan Buddhism. They needed to know that it is not a matter of long and boring rituals or short-term magic, but rather that the methods incorporate a most practical psychology and philosophy with 2500 years of experience behind them. Helping people live, die, and be reborn better, to have meaningful lives, and benefit others, the teachings surely had something to contribute. The perfect material for doing this we carried in five thick hand-written notebooks: the instructions of Kalu Rinpoche in Sonada. They were full of repetitions. He had often started anew when fresh students came, but even that was a useful example. While one should, of course, take inspiration from the highest level of teaching one can understand, it is even more important to solidify the foundation for one's later development. There was surely enough material for a booklet, so we withdrew to our cabin in the Swedish woods to make it happen.

While meditating ten to twelve hours a day on the eighth Karmapa and otherwise only writing and sleeping, a power-field formed around the house. It kept all disturbances away, and one could clearly feel it. On the way to our rustic toilet, situated about 20 meters away from the house, just before reaching the goal of our ardent striving, a large quantity of strange thoughts arose. Returning from the outhouse, at the same distance the protective field enveloped one again. Once more mind became clear, and we could fully focus on the work. Even the friends who came up from Copenhagen on motor-cycles didn't want to chat. They just put the food in the window and left again. From new moon to the day of Black Coat, Mahakala, one day before new moon, we wrote. Then the book, *Teaching on the Nature of Mind,* was finished. It was the first of a half dozen books I wrote on the Buddhist view. Today they culminate in *The Way Things Are,* a mature presentation translated into a score of European languages.

The next pressing concern was money. Due to the fifty German textbooks my father had written, "Nydahl" has a good resonance in the Danish academic world. Thus we quickly got jobs, teaching at a school about sixty kilometers west of Copenhagen. We drove there every morning through the snow and had amazing luck. Despite bald tires and my having to push-start our VW bus on an icy road, we were always right on time. In addition to a full teaching schedule, we worked as night-janitors at another school in Copenhagen itself. Here our friends with questions often came along and helped. With jobs both day and night, we earned good money. It was lots of fun to explode into so much outer activity again.

At no time did we forget that this period in Europe would be of limited duration, that Karmapa would give us a sign when to return East. One day, while Hannah was teaching, I withdrew to a small room in the school to meditate. After some months of saving money, we felt that now again something had to happen. Therefore, I deeply asked Karmapa for direction. While in this state, the door opened and three children carried a large white board up to me. It showed the outline of Asia. No borders, towns, or other sites were marked on the map except for the southern tip of India. Here a large checkered ball had been drawn, and clumsy big letters said ANGALORE. It struck me like lightning: this word could be read as both Bangalore and Mangalore, and between these two major towns lies the southern Tibetan camp. So this should be our next goal. As an extra confirma-tion, on the next morning yet another letter arrived from Ayang

Tulku. He was the lama who had told us about the camps during the great initiation into eight-armed Liberatrice at Rumtek. Once more he asked us to visit him. So the signs were clear, and again we went East. After spending Christmas and New Year's with parents and friends, we packed our rucksacks and left.

CHAPTER SEVENTEEN

The Southern Camps

WE TOOK A CHEAP ARAB FLIGHT via Syria to Bombay; at that time one thought less about what kind of culture one was supporting. Having celebrated instead of sleeping during the last nights, we just woke up a few times for meals and views of desert sand; then it was definitely India. Bombay wasn't easy to get enthusiastic about. While Delhi is angry and Calcutta confused, here pride is king. Therefore, that same evening we took the shaky train to Mysore. From there one reaches the Tibetan camp by bus. All night we rattled along in an overcrowded compartment, and the next day it was necessary to change trains several times, which made it difficult to find rest. Also, having just whisked a lot of gifts through customs without trouble, we didn't want anyone to walk off with them. When changing trains again on the second morning, however, a map showed beyond any doubt that we had hardly left Bombay. It was a deplorable hole in our education not to know that in the western part of the country both buses and steamers make better headway than the trains. The constantly changing landscapes were eye-opening, and one saw many more different races than in the north and east. At nearly every stop, crowds of different-looking people with very different vibrations filled the trains, and only the great new-Indian mantras of "Rupees" and "Paisa" never stopped. Diligently repeated, they stood out in every language and nearly every sentence.

After a further night and morning on the train, we finally arrived in Mysore, on the road between Mangalore and Bangalore. We took a rickshaw pulled by a healthy horse, a rare sight in Asia except for

Afghanistan and the Buddhist countries. As may be expected, Iran is the worst, with skeletons on three stiff legs being whipped to pull the carts in their holy town of Mashad. Having reached the bus terminal with enough oranges for the last hours of the trip, we squeezed into the already overcrowded bus. The feeling in Mysore was unpleasant. Like several other places on the way, they were showing an anti-hippie film, and Indians believe all that they see. It must have been an ugly piece. People clearly didn't like us, and I had to carry some away to clear our seats. After traveling for some hours along alleys with flowering trees, the first Tibetan prayer flags appeared to the right. The sight really struck me, and there was no way I could stop the tears coming to my eyes. I tried to mask my state through fits of coughing and sneezing and looked with great interest out of the window, but actually I was crying. I was just so very happy that Buddhist wisdom and its functioning ways of liberation existed also here. As so often before, a stream of strong promises soon took over. We would do everything for it to survive.

The Indians didn't want Westerners in the camp. Therefore, we didn't get off at the main entrance but drove a few kilometers on. From there, different Tibetans guided us down narrow paths. They led the way through fields and clusters of bushes and trees. With the amount of luggage on our backs, this was a very popular shortcut to the fourth camp, which was the main goal. It was also useful to avoid questions from the Indian officials at the main gate. White people meant money and status, and though they could do nothing to us, there was much local jealousy because of the good practical organization of the refugees. Any situation was welcomed which gave the Indians a lever to control their guests.

It was early in February, and the festivities around Tibetan New Year had not finished. The "Koorg" area where they live is at an altitude of about 1,000 meters, so the nights were still pleasantly cool while the days didn't completely burn one up. The path wound through tightly planted maize fields, so different from those of the locals, and it was evident that the Tibetans, whose diligence we knew, needed only peace to be able to prosper here also.

Camp number four was easy to find. So was house number two, a simple shack made of branches, with an earthen floor. Ayang Rinpoche shared the left half with his three brothers. As always, the

Ayang Tulku with three brothers and monks

early warning system of the Tibetans had functioned well. Soon a group of incredibly well-behaved children brought us to house number eight. It had solid walls and everything was ready to receive us. While a steady stream of delicacies arrived on small plates, most of them digestible to a European, we made a good contact. The lama we would ask for the Phowa teaching had been away for some weeks, but our telegram had been sent after him. Until he returned in a few days, we should stay with his three brothers. They would arrive within a few hours. The forced delay was useful. Thus we became friends with our hosts, could brush up on our rusty Tibetan, and really enjoy their exquisite altar. It filled an entire wall. Though it wasn't quite our tradition, our hosts were from the Sakyapa school, it was good to be surrounded again by Buddha-statues and *thankas*. It was nearly intoxicating to be in a world where so many things had meaning as tools to enlightenment.

After a day of assembling the gifts and showing our hosts how adhesive tape and a typewriter function, the lama came back. His main practice is the above-mentioned Phowa, or "transference of consciousness." We would now be the first Westerners to learn that.

Already the next day, under a single tree in an open field, we started the meditation. I nearly fainted at the first sending up of the mind and, as people came to stare, we broadened the experience in a nearby village. It had the name of the place where Buddha chose to die: Happiness-town, Kushinagar. In a wet and unhealthy, half-finished concrete house, we found what is so rare and precious in India: the peace and quiet to focus properly on something.

The camp of Mundgod lay only a few hours away from the Hippie-Mekka of Goa. Maybe that is why it was kept especially off-limits to Westerners. We took the quick night bus to the stop before the larger town of Hubli, then reached the camp on an early truck full of workers. We had to get there before the Indian police woke up. Unchecked, we walked between the sleeping officials, and the place was not small—from a high point in the landscape near a cooperative shop, twelve villages were visible. Surrounded by fields, they were spread over a large, slightly hilly area of recently cleared jungle.

Somehow the place gave us an unusual feeling. It wasn't just the fluttering prayer flags and a newly built monastery, which of course were a joy to see. The feeling of the area itself was somehow very unique. Gradually we realized the special quality of this camp: we had come to a "whole" world. Here in Mundgod lived a genuine piece of Tibet, something balanced and collectively complete, which we had then only felt among the people from the inner valleys of Bhutan. Although climate and surroundings couldn't have been more opposite to arctic Central Asia, the unbroken power field of old Tibet had been brought here. It still functioned. Disappearing in this camp for six weeks, we would become one with its people and return to human conditions which were always the norm. They lie right below the civilized veneer of this materially endowed present incarnation, which has actually only lasted for 50 years. What we experienced during this time made a lasting impression on our minds, both the very naked conditions under which people lived, as well as the frequently instinctive cooperation displayed. In glimpses, we understood the mechanisms which had allowed vulnerable humanity to survive so many things during so many thousands of years.

An event at this time showed the meaning and power of transmission. During an initiation to Limitless Light, a tuberculosis patient was carried into the room in a sheet. He surely weighed less than sixty pounds. We moved back from the guest carpet and into the flaky dust with everybody else, letting the sick man lie on the softer surface in front. It was a wonder he was alive; there was only skin and bones. Frequently he coughed slime and blood into a cup, which we took care to cover with a piece of paper, while explaining to the people around how the swarms of flies would spread the microbes.

While receiving the blessing of the charged up ritual objects, a visible change took place in his eyes. They radiated more strongly from the inside, while the "pained" lines of his face gradually relaxed. Finally, it was evident that he had entered a state of increasing bliss where he experienced the pure essence of everything around.

Two hours after the initiations, he could go to the mental realm he had waited to enter. He left his destroyed body for great freedom. He now had the ticket to go. The doctors had already written him off a year earlier.

Fewer funny political trips were visible among the Mundgod people than with most central and western Tibetans. They had lots of cultural games, but except for a flare-up of bad gossip when the small, busty women discovered that Nordic Hannah is actually a woman, and I therefore not a monk, they quickly saw the futility of playing any on us. I just didn't care and sometimes badly embarrassed whoever tried. Many had the relaxed good manners signifying inner maturity and worked on from what they had already reached: at sunrise and sunset, from all directions of the camp, one heard the recitation of texts and the crisp sounds of bells and hand drums. Their huts were made of cement or branches and were overcrowded. But in spite of stifling heat, T.B., and poverty, many were fine examples of lay and yogic practitioners. Combining life-experience with the view and methods of the Diamond Way, they were incorporating patterns of behavior that would later deeply inspire the West.

Most of these people came from the western and northern part of Tibet, near Ladakh and Mongolia. They were not the bone-hard Khampa warriors who had brought 85,000 countrymen and most lamas out of Tibet in 1959, but peaceful nomads so far from the cutting edge of events that they were only really targeted after eight years under the Red Chinese. As the cultural revolution cut down on whatever freedom was still left, and they were forced to destroy their places of meditation, about eight thousand had fled penniless via

Nomad-king from Western Tibet;
we stayed with their family

Khampa refugee lady
in the southern camp

Ladakh into India. Under Chinese pressure, the Indians put most on cattle-wagons and transported them to the jungles here, where the funeral pyres burned continually for months. A good 30 percent couldn't survive the alien climate and diseases. In the meantime, the survivors had developed skills in agriculture and were already teaching the Indians. Nearly all of the original inhabitants now had good jobs with the resourceful people from the north.

In the beginning, hordes of elephants had killed quite a few settlers. They liked the jungle the way it was. On walks through the area, people would still point, saying; "Here Tashi was killed; there Dolma was chased." Some had then asked Karmapa to put a protective energy around the settlement, after which the animals didn't come back. We had just heard something similar in Bylakuppe. This camp had also been disturbed by elephants until the Dalai Lama paid a visit.

The camps were a world unto themselves, but it wouldn't stay like that. There were two dangerous signs, the first omens of the decay and hollowing-out of a tradition-based culture. Few young people were around, most had gone to the towns, and electric power was moving in. The masts already stood, the first lines were being drawn; and thus the road was open to distracting, meaningless radio noise and sleepy morning hours. We told them what to watch out for, though maybe not with the greatest conviction. It felt like putting them below ourselves. Tantric practitioners rely on their ability to transform and assimilate things instead of avoiding them. Nothing calls for greater spiritual ripeness and perseverance than this approach, however; it is a super quick but dangerous way. The next years would show if our hosts from Mundgod made it.

Like a few months earlier in Denmark, when the signs had come to visit the southern camps, one day it was time to leave them again. Once more, we felt Karmapa calling, but I also knew that we should first go to Chechoo Rinpoche in Nepal. We took a warm leave of our friends in Mundgod with whom such worlds of experience united us and put our gear on our backs again. As we walked out through the gate after six weeks in the camp, the Indian police stared as if we had fallen down from the sky.

CHAPTER EIGHTEEN

Life—A Dream

KATHMANDU HAD CHANGED LITTLE. The cold fogs of winter were gone, and fields and trees showed the myriad green shades of the valley. The Bodhnath stupa was now "in," and most of our crowd had moved to live around it. They quickly found us a room there too, with a balcony and facing the impressive building itself. After the Phowa, a strong inspiration had repeated itself to now ask Chechoo Rinpoche for the dream meditation, so once again we had some fine days in lively Kathmandu while waiting for our first teacher to return.

During these days of waiting to receive our next meditation, great benefit came from the Phowa already learned. In no time we had attracted the hordes of half-starved dogs living around the stupa. They jumped at absolutely anything that could serve as nourishment, including the excrement of children, and the cheese rinds and pieces of stale bread we threw down to them were especially popular. What they thought of the mantras and good wishes we gave with the food, we never found out, but apparently, they did notice their sponsors. One evening we came back from town very late. As we started to cross the open area from the stupa to our house, as if on signal hordes of dogs came streaming towards us from all sides. In a moment we were surrounded by dozens of them, all barking loudly, and it looked like real trouble. All were sick, and a bite from one of these animals would have been pure poison. I pushed Hannah against the wall of the stupa and pulled out my knife. Then we saw what was going on. With a wave of warmth in our hearts, we realized that they did not want to attack but had actually come to say "Thanks." The rough sounds, which were all they could produce, meant something like, "Thank you for the food." We were deeply touched and strongly wished to be able to do more for these poor animals. The opportunity for this came very soon.

Some people, maybe tourists, had complained about the wild and often rabies-stricken dogs around Bodhnath, and one day a group of policemen appeared. From a sack they threw gray lumps of poisoned meat to the dogs, thus killing them slowly and in great pain. Although the Tibetans tried to hide the dogs they could in their houses, they actually only managed to protect the few who trusted them. Returning in the afternoon, the police had already gone. The result of their work, however, was easy to see. Already at the entrance to the stupa lay a dozen dying dogs, gasping for air. While I sent Hannah for water to quench their thirst, I blessed the dying animals with Karmapa's relics, getting nearly all through to an easy death. The truck which came to pick up the corpses had to wait until I finished, while the Tibetans shared joyfully in what went on.

At that time it became a standing joke that we would get many students with rough voices and long noses, incarnations of the dogs that had died at such a powerful place and with our help.

Then Lama Chechoo came back. It was wonderful to see him again, and he wanted many details of what we had been doing. As I asked him for the dream meditation, he kept looking downward, as if expecting a sign. As it was apparently satisfactory, he quickly glanced up at us in a way we shall never forget and said, "Good, I will give you Milam, the meditation for realizing mind in the dream state."

Even before we heard his "yes," our perception had already changed. Everything became a dream, and that is how it remained for the six weeks we stayed with him. The dream meditation produces a state where whatever "knows," the "observer" is present whether one is awake or asleep. It is like being enormous, transparent, protected space. From this condition, mind learns to recognize its trips and to consciously influence them. One becomes very aware that our so-called waking state is really an individual dream inside a collective one, that the world of one's normal daily consciousness is a set of projections that we share with others. The more similar the view and background, the better the cooperation. This basic difference in perception is clearly why races and cultures mix so badly. As this awareness of radiant space takes root, the disturbing feelings which come from our belief that "things are real" dissolve by themselves.

Thus six weeks passed. We stayed in the dusty storeroom underneath Lama Chechoo, dreamed whether awake or asleep, and constantly felt his power. Several times a day, an exceedingly long-nosed water-rat came to our door. It checked everything, walked at its own quiet pace to the food we had put out for it, picked it up, and walked off again. Except for the rat we had no outside visitors, and the retreat went very deep. Nothing has ever been "narrow" or "boring" since then.

When the practice was finished, Lama Chechoo again manifested in his usual form. It was now again time to go to Karmapa, he said. To get there more quickly and because it only cost nine dollars, we took the flight to Biratnagar, in the very east of Nepal. Chechoo Rinpoche himself drove with us to the airport, and two days later we were already in Sonada, where they knew the exact date of Karmapa's return to Sikkim. Again, Rinpoche had been precise; it was already on the next day.

Sonada was under a black cloud. It was shocking how his community suffered because the lama was not there. Kalu Rinpoche had now been delayed in Canada for over a year, and though they had brought his brother, nothing was happening in the monastery. Such a dependence was touching but also childish, and we decided to do things differently. The goal of Buddhism is becoming independent and finding one's own strength, so this couldn't be the way. In our work in the West, empowering people must be an absolute priority.

The timing was right. We had not been long at the Tista bridge, taking in once again the many worlds crossing there, when Karmapa's cars approached. He smiled, put his finger on my army jacket where the inner pocket held a letter for him which we had completely forgotten, blessed us until we saw light, and happily we got on one of his trucks. Meditating under the beautiful blue sky, we entered Sikkim with him.

The following days in Rumtek were special, and we stayed very aware. We were getting the "junior partner" treatment. Karmapa was letting us look over his shoulder as never before. Many times he showed or told us things which we would not understand until we also became responsible for the development of others. He arranged for us to be there when he gave advice on the running of centers and retreats, when explaining which practices he wanted done and how. Frequently, he asked what we thought, how we would do a thing like that in the West, and he always listened to our ideas but never said "yes" or "no." With certainty, our next meditation or dream would then bring the obvious solution.

One day, when all signs must have been right, and before the Indians started putting on pressure, Karmapa called us to him. He gave our friend Kim Wuensch and us fine, auspicious presents and said that, as the first Westerners, we now had his blessing for starting centers. After the first work in Denmark, I would teach in Europe and everywhere. He promised to guide us and to let his transmission and blessing work through us always. Half in shock but with a burst of energy which is still increasing today, he sent us back to Europe, to the work of this life.

So that was it. In our fever to start, there was no space for doubt or hesitation. The responsibility was intoxicating, and it was no lazy man's job. Bringing liberating teachings to the West while honoring our teachers and the Kagyu Lineage would demand ever increasing awareness. Amazed and with deep gratitude, we noted the many auspicious events gathering in the three weeks until we could get on our overbooked flights from Bombay. They were signs of future success which made joyful sense already then. In Bodh Gaya, taking a hurried leave of the large golden Buddha in the stupa, we both saw it coming alive and actually smiling at us. Totally blasted and running out of the room backwards to catch our motor-scooter before it disappeared with our things, our only thought was, "But he's got a sense of humor." What else was there to think or say?

The vision triggered off a very powerful purification, and the whole way down to Bylakuppe and during the stay there, I was sick as rarely before. It was amazing pain. My head and throat just seemed to explode constantly. Arriving by the pleasant Calcutta-Madras-Mysore trains—there were even seats for everybody—we were just in time for the cementing of the floor in the first building of the new Kagyupa monastery; it lay on a hill with a fine view over the refugee-camp. Though staggering around and dizzy with fever, it felt right to do something in the East before starting in the West, and it was important to know that pain was no obstacle. The local trains up to Bombay again had not picked up speed, but a dozen telegrams from all corners of India had at least preserved our reservation for the flight.

On a cold, clear October evening we landed in the beautiful city of Copenhagen.

CHAPTER NINETEEN

Work Starts

O UR WONDERFUL PARENTS WERE WAITING at the airport, happy
that this time we had not stayed away for years. Around them stood a
fine group of old friends. Several had grown out of the drug-scene at
the time we did, and our first book, *Teachings on the Nature of Mind,*
had influenced them strongly. Due to a rich life-experience and much
good karma, they were now able and willing to benefit others. The
symbolic importance of them standing there was clear, and we were
overjoyed: work in the West would start from the finest basis of all, a
colorful, tested and well-knit group of idealists.

Already on the next evening, Karmapa's transmission awakened
in a group of these friends. With amazement, we understood the
meaning of his last words to us: "I am now with you everywhere and
always." During a beautiful sunset over a Danish bay, for the first time
I transmitted his power on the European continent. Astonished, I
heard myself teach and saw my hands bless those present with
Karmapa's relics. Something far stronger and more conscious than the
"I," which people identify with, pushed its way through, and it was
blissful.

On a larger scale, however, this position meant the gradual
ending of Hannah's and my carefree life as Buddhist consumers. For
one's own life, one may decide to not subject certain values to a critical
analysis. With responsibility for others, however, that luxury is over.

My sequel to this book, *Riding the Tiger* (also Blue Dolphin
Publishing), therefore points out both healthy and unhealthy aspects
of Buddhism coming to the West. Above all, it describes the unique

His Holiness staying at the Copenhagen center, December 1976

development of the liveliest of the settlers: the Karma Kagyu lineage. Recently, Kunzig Shamarpa established the K.I.B.I. Institute in Delhi, Dordogne, Elista, and Virginia. A monastic organization developed in France. Right in the center of life stand, so far, 200 lay and yogic centers around the world, which are my responsibility.

The years of lama-work since 1972 have been thrilling. It has been joyful to see the West absorbing the best from traditional Buddhism, giving it new life in the process.

After 1,250 years, the great prophecy of Guru Rinpoche is fulfilling itself:

"When the fire-ox moves on wheels (trains) and the iron bird flies everywhere (airplanes); when Tibetans are spread like ants around the world, my Dharma will come to the land of the white men."

May liberating and enlightening teachings always reach the bright and independent people, who will use them to benefit others!

List of Tibetan Buddhist Centers

T HE FOLLOWING IS A PARTIAL LIST of the more that 200 centers under the spiritual guidance of the 17th Karmapa Thaye Dorje and the practical direction of Lama Ole Nydahl. For a complete and updated list, visit our website: www.diamondway-buddhism.org

USA

Buddhist Group Albuquerque Central
c/o Kathleen Kess
1321 Fruit Street NW
Albuquerque, NM 87104
Tel: 1-505-247-4723
Email: albqcentral@diamondway.org

Buddhist Group Albuquerque East
c/o Kirsty Mills
Tel: 1-505-291-0717
805 Suzanne Lane SE
Albuquerque, NM 87123
Email: albqeast@diamondway.org

Buddhist Group Austin
c/o Sergio Alay
1509 Nueces Street
Austin, TX 78701
Tel: 1-512-469-7908
Email: austin@diamondway.org

Buddhist Group Boulder
c/o Kevin Rooney
2800 Kalmia, B-312
Boulder, CO 80301
Tel: 1-303-415-9558
Email : boulder@diamondway.org

Buddhist Group Houston
c/o Micheal Savage
4242 Jack St.
Houston, TX 77006
Tel: 1-713-528-5971
Email: houston@diamondway.org

Buddhist Group Clear Lake
c/o Bonnie Cooper
1611 Dakota St.
League City, TX 77573
Tel: 1-281-480-2121
Email: clearlake@diamondway.org

Buddhist Center Los Angeles
c/o Karin Grillitz
432 S. Curzon Av. Apt. 2B
Los Angeles, CA 90036
Tel: 1-213-931-1903
Fax: 1-213-931-0909
Email: losangeles@diamondway.org

Buddhist Group Nevada City
c/o Nancy & Paul Clemens
13386 N. Bloomfield Rd.
Nevada City, CA 95959
Tel: 1-530-265-5044
Fax: 1-530-265-0603

Buddhist Center New York
c/o Lisa & Tasso Kallianiotis
335 Court Place, Suite 137
Brooklyn, NY 11231
Tel: 1-718-858-6578
Fax: 1-212-253-1883
Email: newyork@diamondway.org

Buddhist Group Phoenix
c/o Joe Ciula
4128 N.22nd St. #6
Phoenix, AZ 85016
Tel: 1-602-224-5864
Email: phoenix@diamondway.org

Buddhist Group Portland
c/o Jeri and John Masciocchi
2410 NC Dunckley St.
Portland, OR 97212
Tel: 1-503-281-3631
Fax: 1-53-288-5422
Email: portland@diamondway.org

Buddhist Center San Diego
c/o Diva Clair
271A Hillcrest Dr.
Leucadia, CA 92024
Tel: 1-760-942-4661
Email: sandiego@diamondway.org

Buddhist Center San Francisco
110 Merced Ave.
San Francisco, CA 94127
Tel: 1-415-661-6467
Fax: 1-415-665-2241
Email: sanfrancisco@diamondway.org

Buddhist Group San Luis Obispo
c/o Rosemary Cochran
851 Tulare St.
Pismo Beach, CA 93449
Tel: 1-805-773-3902
Fax: 1-805-773-3902
Email: slo@diamondway.org

Buddhist Group Santa Fe
c/o Paula Brumley
P.O.Box 2959
Santa fe, NM 87505
Tel: 1-505-982-9590
Email: santafe@diamondway.org

AUSTRALIA

Buddhist Group Canberra
c/o Mark Pace
11 Hakea Cres.
O'Connor, ACT 2602
Tel + Fax: 61-6-6257 7982
Email: markpace@ozemail.com.au

Buddhist Group Perth
c/o Shona & Stewart Jarvis
90a Waddell Road
Bicton, Perth, WA 6156
Tel: 61-8-9319 2616
Email: stewartj@faroc.com.au

Buddhist Center Sydney
c/o Donald Marshall
99 Gowrie Street
Newtown, (Sydney), NSW 2042
Tel + Fax: 61-2-9557 3275
Email: Itay@ozemail.com.au

CANADA

Buddhist Group Calgary
c/o Carl White and Nicholas Jones
226 - 25 Ave. S.W.
Calgary, Alberta T2S 0L1
Tel: 1-403-229-9081
Fax: 1-403-262-3623
Email: jonesele@telusplanet.net

Buddhist Center Edmonton
c/o Janice + Paul Pype
11643 - 111A Avenue
Edmonton, Alberta T5G 0G2
Tel: 1-403-447-1845
Email: ppype@connect.ab.ca

Buddhist Group Vancouver
c/o Jolanta Pyra
201-1230 E. 8th Ave.
Vancouver, BC V5T1V2
Tel: 1-604-876-3875
Fax: 1-604-876-9697
Email: kclvancouver@hotmail.com

UNITED KINGDOM

Buddhist Center London
c/o Anthony Hopson & Filitz Regvan
Flat 11, 51 Tudor Road
UK Hackney, E9 7SN
Tel + Fax: 44-181-5251821
Email: diamondway@
buddhismlondon.demon.co.uk

Buddhist Group Cambridge
c/o Marieke Stevens
30 Belgrave Road
UK Cambridge CB1 3DE
Tel: 44-1223-521904

AUSTRIA

Karme Tschö Ling Wien
Josef Melichargasse 20
A-1210 Wien
Tel: 43-1-2631247
Fax: 43-1-2631246
Email: sanghahaus@blackbox.at

COLOMBIA

Buddhist Center Bogotá
c/o Eduardo Velazquez
Tel: 57-3-2183315
Email: evl@colomsat.net.co

DENMARK

Buddhist Center København
Svanemøllevej 56
DK-2100 København Ø
Tel: 45-39 292711
Fax: 45-39 295733
Email: kdl-cph@post1.tele.dk

GERMANY

Buddhist Center Wuppertal
Heinkelstr. 27
D-42285 Wuppertal
Tel: 49-202-84089
Fax: 49-202-82845
Email: 100671.2041@
compuserve.com

Buddhist Center Hamburg
Thadenstr. 79
22767 Hamburg
Tel: 49-171-98 21 21 9
Fax: 49-40-43 25 43 31
Email: 100600.3234@
compuserve.com

HOLLAND

Buddhist Center Amsterdam
Michel van Dinteren &
Jody den Besten
Tweede Schinkelstraat 20c
NL-1075 TT Amsterdam
Tel + Fax: 31-20-6792917
Email: kagyuams@worldonline.nl

HUNGARY

Buddhist Center Budapest
c/o Eva & István Gruber
Buday László u. 7
H-1024 Budapest
Tel + Fax: 36-1-2741006
Email: 100324.435@
compuserve.com

NEW ZEALAND

Buddhist Group Christchurch
c/o Manfred Ingerfeld
37 Melrose Street
Christchurch
Tel: 64-3-3658221
Email: M.Ingerfeld@
botn.canterbury.ac.nz

POLAND

Buddhist Retreat Kuchary
Kuchary 57
PL-09-210 Drobin
Tel + Fax: 48-24-2601056
Email: kuchary@micronet.com.pl

RUSSIA

Buddhist Center Petersburg
c/o Sasha Koibagarov
ul. Varshavskaya 16 - 17
196 105 St. Petersburg
Tel + Fax: 7-812-2963468
Email: sashaakk@mail.nevalink.ru

SPAIN

Buddhist Retreat Karma Guen
Atalaya Alta
Apartado 179
E-29700 Velez-Malaga
Tel: 34-95-2030352
Fax: 34-95-2115197
Email: cyberdorje@earthling.net

SWITZERLAND

Buddhist Center Zürich
Hammerstr. 9a
CH-8008 Zürich
Tel: 41-1-3820875
Fax: 41-1-3800144
Email: 100553.3425@
compuserve.com

VENEZUELA

Buddhist Center Caracas
c/o Dilia, Mazo & Arturo Navarro
P.O. Box 88520
Caracas 1080
Tel + Fax: 58-2-9458669
Email: ckc-caracas@iname.com

Index

removing suffering, 48
See also Bodhisattva vow;
    Bodhisattvas; healing others
Herat (Afghanistan): Ole's memories
    of, 43–44
Himalayas:
    Kanchenjunga range, 108, 138
    money exchanges in, 78
    O&H's mountain climbing trip,
      66–76
    O&H's Sherpa Country trip, 77–99
    Ole's first sight of, 4
    trees, 70, 79
    See also Everest, Mount
Hindu gurus:
    O&H's impressions of, 6
    swami of Delhi, 47–49
      disciple John, 94
Hindus in Nepal, 70
    houses, 83
      as closed to O&H, 69, 70, 79
    Ranas caste, 67
horse caravan: O&H's trek with, 83,
    87
horsefly: Ole's killing of, 89–90
horses: treatment of workhorses in
    Nepal, 18, 83
houses in Nepal:
    of Hindus, 83
      as closed to O&H, 69, 70, 79
    in Kathmandu, 12–13
    of Sherpas, 83, 92
human beings: state (level) of existence,
    144
hundred-syllable mantra: O&H's
    practice of, 164, 172–175
hungry ghosts: state (level) of existence,
    144

I
"I" (ego):
    dissolution of, 170, 171
    as the observer, 205
    rebirth of a separate "I", 142, 146,
      172
ignorance:
    life and suffering as arising from,
      146, 172–173
    removing, 48

illusion of separateness: life and
    suffering as arising through,
    146, 172
impermanence: Kalu Rinpoche's
    teachings on, 147
impressions (karmic), 48
    creation of: conditions for, 173
    results, 173–174
      worlds of rebirth from, 142–143,
      174
    transforming, 116, 132
      O&H's engagement in, 175, 188
      steps in the process, 174
incarnations (of lamas):
    Dukpa lama, 49, 74
    embarrassments in the West, 112–
      113
    Karmapas, 122, 150, 191
      lineage holders, 16, 60
    recognition of as boys, 51, 151, 177,
      185
    young rinpoches with Karmapa, 60,
      179
      O&H and, 178
    See also Dalai Lama; Karmapa;
      Kunzig Shamarpa Rinpoche;
      tulkus
India:
    Bihar, 9
    Bodh Gaya, 49–50
    Bombay, 197
    Calcutta, 143, 163, 197
    cars, 107
    caste system, 106
    Chinese pressure on, 124, 171
    Ghoom, 107, 109
    Kalimpong, 125, 128, 160
    Kurseong, 107
    Ladakh, 95
    Mysore, 197–198
    and Nepal: political relations, 30
    O&H's travel in, 9, 47, 105–109,
      125–134
      Bodh Gaya, 49–50, 207
      Calcutta trips, 143, 163
      Puri, 163–164
      Tibetan refugee camps in the
        south, 195–196, 197–203
    overpopulated lowlands, 105, 155

Palmo, Sister, 112–113, *113*
  eighth Karmapa meditation
    instructions, 191
patience: as a liberating action, 180
Pema Jungne. *See* Guru Rinpoche
penicillin without contraceptives:
    consequences in India, 105, 155
Phowa practices (consciousness
    transference), 39–40, 171,
    176–177, 200–201
  O&H's initiation, 199–200
  as put to use, 176–177, 200–201,
    204–205
Phunchoeling (Bhutan): O&H's stay
    in, 129–131, 133
plays: Retreat of the Rains ceremonial
    dances, 117–120
Pokhara (Nepal), 17–18
Polo, Marco: and Karma Pakshi, 122
porters in Nepal, 71–72, 73
  dealing with, 70, 75–76
  walking techniques, 71, 73–74
practice:
  motivation for, 147, 178–180
    O&H's sense of, 175, 188
  O&H's formal practice needs, 122,
    141
  O&H's joy in, 175, 183, 188
  O&H's practice without a Refuge
    ceremony, 89, 176
  six liberating actions, 180–181
  tantric, 203
  See also ceremonies; foundation
    practices (Kagyu); mantras;
    meditation; Phowa practices
pride:
  impressions of: world of rebirth
    from, 143
  life and suffering as arising through,
    146, 172–173
prophecy of Guru Rinpoche, 210
prostrations:
  benefits, 148–149, 158–159
  O&H's practice of, 148–150, 158–
    160
  traditional, 114
protectors (*Cheuchong*) (Buddha-
    energies), 116
  invocation of, 164–165

  procession of, *169*
  wrathful forms, 56, 116
  See also Black Coat; Mahakala
protectors (*sungdue*), 28, 34, 38
  See also medicine packages
pujas, 61–62, 123
Punlop Rinpoche: and O&H, 65
Puntsho (monk): and O&H, 17
Pure Land:
  invocation at death, 170, 189
  meditation practice, 39–40, 171
Puri (India):
  Australian couple from, 166
  O&H's trip to, 163–164
purification practices. *See* foundation
    practices (Kagyu)

R
radio: Ole's repair of, 120
rain:
  Kalu Rinpoche and the alcoholic
    Sherpas, 185–186
  and Karmapa, 120
rainmaking lama, 28, 97
rains retreat. *See* Retreat of the Rains
    (Yerne)
Ranas caste in Nepal: cars, 67
Rangjung dorje (third Karmapa): and
    Dzogchen, 150
rebirth:
  of lamas: Karmapa's confirmations
    of, 151, 177
  of the mind:
    impressions and, 142–143, 173–
      174
    separate "I", 142, 146, 172
  See also reincarnation
Red Hat schools of Diamond Way
    Buddhism:
  and Guru Rinpoche, 92
  Phowa (consciousness transference)
    practices, 39–40, 171, 176–
    177, 199–200, 200–201
  vs. Yellow Hat school, 92, 161–162
Refuge (in Diamond Way Buddhism),
    91, 114–116
Refuge ceremony:
  O&H's initiation, 112–114
  O&H's practice without, 89, 176

Sherpas:
    near Darjeeling: Kalu Rinpoche and,
        185
    of Nepal:
        earthy practices, 91
        fireplaces, 94
        food, 93–94
        history, 91
        houses, 83, 92
        O&H's overnights with, 80, 84
        statues, 82, 92
        thankas, 82
        traits, 83, 94
Sikkim:
    O&H's travel to, 99, 101, 103–111,
        166, 191
    Tibetan border incidents, 124
    whiskey advertisements, 110
Siliguri (India), 106–107
silver bracelets bought by O&H, 21
Situ Rinpoche, 60, 178, *179*
six liberating actions (of Bodhisattvas),
    180–181
six worlds. *See* worlds (states of
    existence)
smoke: lamas and, 151–152
soil erosion in Nepal, 70
Sonada (India), 107, 134
    community suffering in Kalu
        Rinpoche's absence, 206
    O&H's friends' visit to, 187
    O&H's move to, 138, 141, 143
    O&H's stay in, 143, 158, 166, 172,
        183, 187, 188, 191
    war-related changes, 188
statues:
    of the Buddha:
        Bodh Gaya Buddha, *48*, 207
        Joy-Buddha of Swayambhu
            Temple, *14*, 16
        largest in the world, 5
    roadside statues, 79
    robbery of, 84–85
    of the Sherpas, 82, 92
    smashed by Chinese, 84
stupas:
    Bodh Gaya stupa, *48*
    circumambulating, 85
    near Jumbesi, 85, 92

parts and aspects of, 85–86
roadside stupas, 79
significance, 13, 16, 63, 85
See also Bodhnath stupa
stupidity:
    impressions of: world of rebirth
        from, 143
    life and suffering as arising through,
        146, 172–173
Sue and Richard (Diamond Way
    students), 138, 148
suffering:
    eight sufferings, 144
    as an incentive to practice, 147
    Kalu Rinpoche's teachings on, 147
    origins, 146
    removing, 48, 173
        See also healing others; helping
            others
    working with pain, 178
sungdue. See protectors (*sungdue*)
Swayambhu Temple (Kathmandu),
    15–17
    Chenrezig *thanka, 81*
    Karmapa at, 51–54, 61–65
    stairs up to, *17*
Swiss:
    as immigrants in Nepal, 79
    Tibetan refugee camp efforts, 18

T
Tai Situpa. *See* Situ Rinpoche
taking refuge. *See* Refuge (in Tibetan
    Buddhism); Refuge ceremony
Tamang people: O&H's stay with,
    155–156
tantric practice, 203
Tantric Tibetan Buddhism. *See*
    Diamond Way Buddhism
Tara. *See* Dolkar (White Liberatrice);
    Dolma (Green Liberatrice)
Tashi (of the Gompus Hotel), 128,
    160–161, 162
Tashkent (Kazakhstan), 25
Taxindu monastery, 97
teachers. *See* lamas
Teaching on the Nature of Mind (Ole
    Nydahl), 194–195
Tenga Rinpoche, *168*

vows, 178
  Bodhisattva vow, 178–182
  O&H's vows to help others, 90,
    114–115, 178–182

W

walking techniques in mountain
  climbing, 73–74
walls (path dividers) (mani): significance of, 86–87
The Way Things Are (Ole Nydahl),
  173, 195
Westerners: Karmapa and, 119
  See also friends of O&H (Western)
Wheel of Life, *145*
White Liberatrice. *See* Dolkar
wisdom:
  five wisdoms as represented in
    stupas, 85–86
  as a liberating action, 181
women:
  of Afghanistan, 43
  of India, 9
  of Moslem countries, 9, 43, 46
  of Nepal, 9, 79
  of Pakistan, 46
  of Russia, 25
  See also dakinis (women of wisdom)
worlds (states of existence):
  characteristics, 144–146
  rebirth into, 142–143, 173–174
wrathful deities. *See* protectors
  (*Cheuchong*) (Buddha-energies)
Wuensch, Kim: teaching authorization
  from Karmapa, 207

Y

Yellow Hat school of Diamond Way
  Buddhism: vs. Red Hat
  schools, 92, 161–162
Yerne. *See* Retreat of the Rains
yidam, 115
Yogi Chen. *See* Chen, Yogi
yogini near Mount Everest, 97

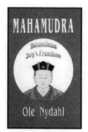